down the road a piece

Annie's Book Stop
676 Post Rd. # 7
Wells, Maine 04090
(207) 646-3821
www.anniesbookstopwells.com

Also from John McDonald

A Moose and a Lobster Walk into a Bar: Tales from Maine

Also from Islandport Press

Mary Peters

Nine Mile Bridge: Three Years in the Maine Woods

The Cows Are Out! Two Decades on a Maine Dairy Farm

Silas Crockett

In Maine

Land of the Porcupine: Growing up in Madawaska

Those Damned Yankees:
The Not-So-Great History of Baseball's Evil Empire

Hauling by Hand: The Life and Times of a Maine Island

The Story of Mount Desert Island

Children's Books from Islandport Press

Titus Tidewater

When I'm With You

down the road a piece
A Storyteller's Guide to Maine

John McDonald

ISLANDPORT PRESS • FRENCHBORO • NEW GLOUCESTER

Islandport Press
Auburn Hall, Suite 203
60 Pineland Drive
New Gloucester, Maine 04260
207.688.6290

www.islandportpress.com

ISBN: 0-9763231-3-3
Library of Congress Control Number: 2005937113

First edition published December 2005
Second edition published June 2007

Book design by Islandport Press Inc.
Book cover design by Karen Hoots/Mad Hooter Design
Cover photograph by Fred J. Field
Illustrations by Leslie Mansmann

To Rebecca and Michael,
as you begin your journey together.

Acknowledgments

Once again I am indebted to the Maine newspapers that carry my weekly column and therefore give me regular incentives to sit down and write. If your newspaper doesn't carry the column, I'd appreciate it if you'd do me a favor and ask the editor why. Anyway, without newspapers and the people who regularly pick them up and read them, people like me might be forced to go out and do something else—like work.

Dean Lunt and Amy Canfield of Islandport Press deserve thanks for their skill at making what I pound out on my computer a little more understandable. You should see this stuff in its original form!

I'd also like to thank the thousands of people—from here and from away—who plunked down their hard-earned money to buy my first Islandport book, *A Moose and a Lobster Walk into a Bar*. That book took off when it hit bookstores in the fall of 2002 and, judging from my latest royalty check, it's still doing a decent job of getting itself sold. Buying that first book may not have been a big deal for those readers, but it was pretty important to me. If it wasn't for all those people buying all those books, this latest effort you're reading now probably wouldn't exist, and you'd sure look funny standing here in this bookstore holding an imaginary book in your hands.

I'd also like to thank—once again—the friendly professionals at libraries in Oxford Hills and Portland who helped me with research and fact checking. As Mark Twain said: Always begin with the facts; you can misconstrue them as you wish later.

While in the thank-you mode, we might as well give a tip-of-the-hat and a sincere thanks to all those people who staff our road-repair crews, all the fun-loving folks "from away," especially those who own and drive monstrous motor homes, and the special individuals who operate establishments like B&Bs. These selfless people work tirelessly to help keep Maine humor alive. Most are good sports, able to chuckle along here with the rest of us.

I hope this is enough to get these people to buy this book in great numbers for themselves and as gifts for all their friends.

Thanks, folks.

This is also the place to acknowledge the love and support of my wife Ann who has encouraged me—in her strong, determined way—to get this book written.

John McDonald
Portland, Maine
November 2005

Contents

But First, Let Me Just Say This

Forget all the modern techie stuff available to twenty-first-century travelers—Internet maps, Global Positioning Systems, cell phones, and so forth. This tour book will re-create for you the spirit of the olden days here in Maine, when Men were Men—and probably lost. In olden days helpless tourists stopped to ask directions from natives at their own peril. The only alternative was to rely on the state's notoriously quirky road signs—leastways those signs that weren't riddled with buckshot or removed entirely to decorate the local lodge or teenager's bedroom.

Meaning this book will give you that same uneasy feeling: What to believe? What not to believe?

This book also comes in the new state-mandated spirit of actually *helping* tourists rather than simply toying with them for one's own amusement. After all, it is no secret that in parts of our fair state, toying with visitors is one of the only forms of guaranteed-to-please summer entertainment available. In fact, Maine's reputation in this regard is so bad, the state's tourist authorities issued a pamphlet to natives with tips on how they could best help summer visitors enjoy themselves. The so-called goal was to project a more friendly and welcoming image so that even more tourists would come and—and this is the Holy Grail of state tourism planning—spend even more of their money.

Necessary? Probably; but by my reckoning, our previous alleged ignorance of the proper way to treat a tourist didn't prompt any of them to turn around at the border or even slow the flow of them into the state.

As long as I can remember, starting around Memorial Day Weekend—aka, The Unofficial Start of the Tourist Season—people from away start pouring into our beautiful state in search of Moose, Lobsters, and Lighthouses (MLL) and other attractions in such overwhelming numbers that in some of our more popular resort areas, their numbers rival the number of blackflies and mosquitoes—combined.

Given the sheer numbers of tourists, the size of their bulging wallets, and the need to move even more Maine T-shirts and crafts out of the state, tourism officials began to formally review our state's policies—both written and unwritten—on summer visitors.

The results were stunning. Apparently, according to an economic analysis by a gang of unbiased tourism consultants, every $1 of state tax money invested in the Tourist Industry (you know it has gotten big when it becomes an Industry) returns no less than $1 zillion and fifty scratch lottery tickets to the state coffers. That is definitely true, because there is no way a highly paid group of handpicked consultants would exaggerate or skew results.

So, believe you me, we now have all kinds of policies on you people as we work to better nurture, develop, and expand our hospitality businesses.

(In the spirit of disclosure, I should probably confess that I just violated one of those policies—the one that says natives should avoid referring to you people as "you people" whenever possible. I guess they are trying to get away from the us-versus-them mindset, but sometimes it's unavoidable. By my reckoning, "you people" is still more enlightened than other terms, such as Summer Complaints or #%@$& Jerks.)

The current rule is that from Memorial Day to Labor Day (and now even into the oddly coined Shoulder Seasons), the tourist is The Most Important Person in the State—regardless of whether they are using cash, check, or major credit card. For example, if it came down to the choice of a) directing an elderly woman to an emergency room for life-saving treatment or b) personally driving a tourist to the nearest clam shack for emergency fried clams and a Coke, you should without a moment's hesitation head for the clam shack.

We Mainers have been strongly urged to remember that tourists are not dependent on us; we are dependent on them. We must never make a tourist *feel* dependent, and must never use a lost tourist for sport even if—more than likely—they are from Massachusetts. When they interrupt you to ask for directions to some popular, overpriced destination that you could never hope to afford—say, someplace like Meddybemps on the Machias—avoid the temptation to direct them in circles just to see if they're clever enough to follow directions, and then see how long it takes them to figure out what you're doing.

In another example, avoid this scenario:

Tourist: "What's the quickest way to Bangor?
You: "Are you going by car?"
Tourist: "Yes."
You: "Well, that's the quickest way."

Likewise, avoid this exchange:

Tourist: "Excuse me, sir. I'm on my way to Ellsworth; does it make any difference which way I go at this fork in the road?"
You: "Not to me it don't."

And this:

Tourist: "Excuse me, sir. Where does this road go?"
You: "This road don't go nowhere. It mostly just sets right here."

I make fun, but it is an economic fact that with the worming, clear-cutting, and garden ornament industries all struggling, tourism is critical to the state. So I don't blame the state's tourism people for taking the hospitality business very seriously; someone should. And some of those tourism people even go to college for a hospitality degree, studying for four long years how to make change from a twenty-dollar bill, show people to room 221, act polite, and practice saying, "Do you want fries with that?"

I may not have such a fancy type of college degree, but I figured I'd do my part to boost the state's tourism industry and help liberate tourists from their money by writing this guide. And I'll keep you, our beloved tourists, in mind throughout. Respectfully, of course.

If I remember correctly, it was the legendary Leon L. Bean of Freeport, a man who knew a thing or two about dealing profitably with folks from away, who would tell his employees, "A customer is not someone to argue or match wits with. Nobody ever won an argument with a customer."

I believe old L.L. also said that matching wits with some folks from away is like dueling with an unarmed man—but surely he never said it within earshot of paying customers.

It wouldn't have been hospitable.

Introduction to Maine

Maine is the largest of the six New England states, roughly equal in size to the other five combined. It is mostly bounded by the Gulf of Maine, the St. Croix River, New Brunswick, the St. John River and Quebec. It is also the only state in the Union bordered by only one other state. Unfortunately for Maine, that state is New Hampshire.

Trees cover nearly 90 percent of the land, which is a patchwork of unspoiled rustic woods, majestic mountains, bold granite coasts, and trailer parks. It is a land of clambakes and scratch tickets, of hunting, fishing, sailing, hiking, spray-painted traffic signs, discount outlets, and bait shops.

The harsh, unforgiving weather has given rise to a hardy, humble, independent-minded breed blessed with common sense and a can-do attitude compared to their spleeny, sissy neighbors in Southern New England. Maine natives are frugal, proud, family-oriented, and loyal.

The state motto is "Maine—the way life should be." If you were to personally dispute that in front of a native, he or she is just apt to shut off the cable, put down the Doritos, push aside the bowl of Grapenut ice cream, get up off the sectional, and give you a wicked harsh tongue-lashing. So you'd better just accept our motto and be done with it.

What to call a person from Maine

Many visitors often ask, "What do you call someone from Maine?" People from New York are New Yorkers, people from the United States are Americans, people from Canada are hockey players, people from Vermont are weird—so what do you call people from Maine? There are actually many words used to describe Maine people—many not printable in this family guide—but the most common are Down Easters, Mainiacs, and Mainers. I think Mainiac has a good, authentic ring to it, but most people nowadays say Mainer.

The origins of the name Maine

Another frequently asked question is: "Why do you call this state Maine? Was it named after someone? Was there a Mr. Maine?"

You might hear some snappy answers, all correct, like: "'Cause we want to," or "Well, New Jersey was already taken," or "We call it Maine because our parents called it Maine and their parents called it Maine and their parents called it Maine, so don't come around here and try and cause trouble." A Mainer might also give you a queer look and just say nothing (a common response, actually, to many questions from flatlanders).

The honest-to-gosh truth is: We have no idea, but not knowing something has never stopped a Mainer or an academic from plowing ahead.

One popular theory is that our state was named after the province of Mayne in France. That sounds reasonable, except that Fernando Gorges and John Mason—the two old English sea dogs who were granted the original charter to these lands in 1622—weren't French, had no known connection to France, probably hated France and, therefore, had little reason to hang the name of a French province on this particular piece of real estate.

Yet, other historians (already tenured, I hope) discovered that Mason had once been stationed in the Orkney Islands, where the main island is also called Maine. Did Mason decide to name his new piece of land after an island in the Orkneys? (And, just what kind of name is Orkney, anyway?) Or was it because Gorges's family came from a village, which neighbored Broadmayne, which at various times was known as Maine, Meine, Chow Mein, Lo Chow Mein, and part of it as Parva Maen ("Little Maine").

Others claim that because there are so many islands off our coast that were being used for a variety of reasons, the name Maine is simply a nautical term that refers to the "mainland."

Could be. We just don't know, because no one said. That's right! The reason we don't know why our state is called Maine is because neither Mason nor Gorges ever wrote down and explained why they were giving this place that particular name. The Mainiacs.

Maine Facts

Statehood:	March 15, 1820. Maine joined the Union as the 23rd state as part of the Missouri Compromise.
State Capital:	Augusta or DiMillo's Floating Restaurant in Portland. A coin flip, really.
State Motto:	Dirigo, which means "I Lead." Sometimes mistakenly thought to be "Ayuh" or "Shop L.L. Bean!"
State Nickname:	Officially, Pine Tree State. Unofficially, Yard Sale Capital of the Northeast.
State Bird:	Chickadee
State Tree:	Eastern White Pine
State Flower:	White Pinecone and Tassel
State Animal:	Moose. Hey, this ain't no beauty contest.
State Cat:	Maine Coon Cat
State Berry:	Wild Blueberry
Population:	1,274,923—about a gazillion times that in the summer.
Cities:	22—but take that with a grain of salt.
Towns:	424
Plantations:	51
Unorganized Townships:	416—Really! One day we'll try and get them all sorted out.
Miles of Rivers and Streams:	More than 5,000 rivers and more than 32,000 miles of inland waterways. So, you might ask, why is it that a teensy-weensy, itty-bitty stretch of the Saco River is always bumper-to-bumper with canoes, tubes and six-packs? It's a mystery.
Lakes and Ponds:	6,000
Persons per Square Mile:	41.3. I believe the .3 person is a transplant from Cambridge, Mass.
Coastline:	3,500 miles
Moose Population:	We have about 30,000 or so, give or take.
Lobster Population:	There is some debate here. Scientists and the Academic Crowd claim there is exactly *one* lobster

left in the entire world and that the record number of lobsters being caught by fishermen is just an illusion. Meanwhile, fishermen say that lobsters are piled ass-deep on the ocean bottom, and that no matter how many traps they use or how many people fish for them, the supply will never be exhausted. Let's agree to disagree, I'd say, and enjoy a nice lobster dinner.

Area: Maine has about 33,215 square miles of total area. And we are downright proud of the fact that a handful of those 33,215 square miles are still owned by actual Maine people. At least that's the rumor.

Distances: As the seagull flies, Maine stretches 311 miles north to south and 202 miles east to west. But if you drive actual Maine roads, it is roughly 176,780 miles north to south and 156,005 miles east to west—if you know the shortcuts and can avoid the potholes.

Highest Point: Mount Katahdin, 5,268 feet

Counties: Maine has 16 counties; 14 that actually count.

Time Zone: Sunup to sundown

Radar Detectors: Permitted (but not encouraged)

Firearms Laws: Maybe, but none's so you notice. Most likely another rumor.

Fishing & Hunting: Ayuh.

Taxes: We have every shape and manner of tax imaginable. If it exists in solid, liquid or gas form, we tax it; if it moves, we tax it even more; if it breathes, we tax it the most; and when it finally dies—just for good measure—we tax it again.

Major Industries: Tourism, lobster fishing, logging, paper, tourism, Wal-Mart, worming, yard sales, painting on shells and rocks, and pothole filling.

Political system

Ask some people and they'll tell you that Maine has a strong two-party political system. Ask other people the same question and they'll say Maine has no organized political parties—just Democrats and Republicans. There is also rumored to be something called the Green Party in Maine, but I think essentially it's just a couple of kids laid off from the coffeehouse looking for seasonal work.

It has not always been like this. Years ago Maine was one of the most Republican states in the nation. That is no longer the case, but back when it was, and folks in my hometown of Cherryfield would have an election and then go down to town hall to count up the ballots, the total would always be: Republicans, 293 votes; Democrats, 0.

I remember back when Democrat John F. Kennedy ran for president against Richard Nixon. I wasn't old enough to vote, but I followed the day-to-day campaign closely. On election night I went down to town hall to watch the ballot counting, and as they went through the pile it was one Republican vote after another.

Then, about halfway through the pile they came across a ballot marked KENNEDY. The smoothly running process came to a screeching halt as a poll official fished out the unusual ballot and passed it around the table for all to examine.

"Where'd *that* come from," asked First Selectman Arthur Strout.

"I don't know," said clearly annoyed Third Selectman Sherm Ames.

As the curious ballot went around the table, almost everyone had a snide comment about who may have cast the vote, but in the end they begrudgingly concluded that the ballot looked legal and therefore probably had to be counted.

Continuing the count, all the remaining ballots were landing in the Republican pile until they came to the second-to-last one, and darned if it wasn't another marked KENNEDY.

Well, that's all Second Selectman Ed Beal could stand. He jumped to his feet, grabbed the offending ballot and said: "The son of a bitch must have voted twice!"

So, they ripped up both errant ballots and the final vote—as usual—was Republicans 293. Democrats 0.

Maine Regions in Brief

Southern zone (North Massachusetts)

When you cross the bridge into Kittery you are technically in Maine, but don't believe it. Many Mainers don't consider York County part of Maine, and if New Hampshire offered to trade us a box of taffy and a piece of the White Mountains we'd take the deal and wash our hands of that whole pointy end of the state. It's mostly sand, anyway, and here in Northern New England we have a fondness for rocks over sand.

Portland zone

Some people—mostly flatlanders who now live in Portland—like to divide Maine into two distinct parts: Greater Portland and Lesser Maine. They point to all the usual stuff—Portland's fine museums, art galleries, theaters, and trendy restaurants. But you can't get them to shut up, so they go on and on about Portland's historic architecture, quaint neighborhoods, and islands. And did I mention the trendy restaurants?

All that talk must be working because Portland is one of the most popular places in Maine, and if you don't believe it, just ask someone from there. Portland attracts many younger people from throughout the state (and of course, those looking for an actual job) who arrive there first to go to places like the University of Southern Maine, and then stay because of those hip little restaurants that serve strange foods most Mainers wouldn't talk about (at least in polite company), never mind eat at or afford.

That's the good news.

The bad news is that members of the criminal class from as far away as Massachusetts and beyond are also attracted to Portland, allowing it to lead the state in things like crime, drug use, confiscatory rents, and lawyers.

For those who like to live life fast (as opposed to half-fast), you'll be glad to know that Portland will take your money faster and max out your credit cards quicker than any other place in Northern New England.

Mid-coast zone

To be fair, there is considerable debate here. Some say the mid-coast stretches from Brunswick to Bucksport, and some say it goes from Waldoboro to Camden or Bath to Belfast. You might as well have your say. Just pick any two towns on the coast between Kittery and Calais, and that can be your mid-coast.

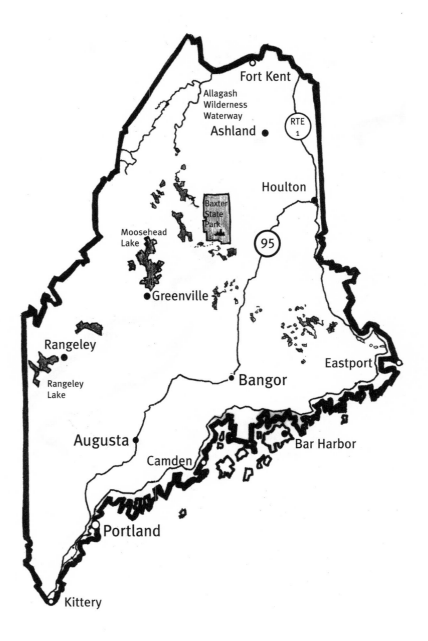

Fort Kent

Allagash
Wilderness
Waterway

RTE
1

Ashland

Houlton

Baxter
State
Park

Moosehead
Lake

95

Greenville

Rangeley

Eastport

Rangeley
Lake

Bangor

Augusta

Bar Harbor

Camden

Portland

Kittery

Real Maine zone

As much a state of mind as a geographical area.

The Real Maine zone has many tentacles that can extend into the darnedest and hardest-to-reach places. You'll think you're in the middle of the trendy Greater Portland zone or some other fashionable place and suddenly you'll come upon something like the Maine Idyll Motor Court in Freeport or a nice trailer park and whew, just like that, you're in the Real Maine.

Time was when most of Maine was a Real Maine zone and you had to look hard to find a place that wasn't. Back in the 1950s some used to think that Monhegan Island, with all its beatniks and New York artists, wasn't part of Real Maine, but of course it was. Maine has always been home to the art crowd and those who like to hang around where artists hang around.

You'll know you're in the Real Maine zone if the mailbox in front of the house looks like a lobster trap, or if there's a mailbox on a 12-foot pole labeled AIR MAIL. (Once I even saw one of those 12-foot-high boxes marked BILLS.)

The Real Maine zone includes dooryards with old cars, furniture, appliances, engine blocks hanging from tripods, and lots of other useful things that real Mainers don't like to throw out for fear of needing them later on. You'll also find some of the finest, most clever lawn ornaments on the planet.

Former summer complaints who become year-round residents like to pass local laws banning real dooryards, calling them eyesores and worse. That's only one reason why the Real Maine zone is slowly disappearing before our eyes.

If you see a real Maine dooryard while driving around, stop your car immediately and get a picture of it. Chances are it won't be there when you come back through.

You know you are in Real Maine if:

- Houses leave their Christmas lights up year-round and take the wreath down only for the Fourth of July.
- There is an honest-to-goodness, authentic barbershop.
- The "Day Spa" is in a double-wide.
- You see lots of signs that say FILL WANTED.
- There are more Dunkin' Donuts than Starbucks.
- You can buy vegetables outside someone's house on the *honor* system—and people leave money.
- The radio stations all play country music.

Scenic zone

It's not bragging to say that Maine has some of the most junk-filled dooryards of any place in the country. The beauty of Maine is that we also have some of the most magnificent scenery in the world—and that's not bragging because it's true. The millions of people who visit Acadia National Park every year don't come just for the overpriced, Chinese-made souvenirs and stuffy B&Bs. If asked, most would say they come for the scenery.

Acadia might be the most popular of Maine's scenic attractions, but there are many others, and some don't even charge admission. From across Frenchman Bay, for example, in places like Lamoine and Sullivan, you can get a spectacular view of Acadia without having to sit in fume-choked lines of traffic.

I used to wonder if New Hampshire had more scenic places (until the Old Man of the Mountain fell and couldn't get up) than we did, what with their fancy White Mountains and all.

Then I realized that it was all a clever optical illusion. It's just because New Hampshire is so much smaller than Maine, and they do have those mountains, which I admit are impressive, that it *seems* like they have more scenery. But they don't.

We may not have their Presidential Range, but we do have Mount Katahdin and quite a few other impressive mountains that—if you are one of those people who love to know such trivia—are over four thousand feet high.

And of course we have the Maine Coast. New Hampshire has Portsmouth.

Penobscot Bay zone

When people think of sailing the coast of Maine they're usually thinking about a sunny August day on Penobscot Bay, which stretches from Monhegan in the west to Swans Island in the east. Besides having the standard rocky coast, this area also has added attractions like the Camden Hills, Blue Hill, and the peaks of Mount Desert Island.

Down East zone

Our state slogan is: "Maine—the way life should be." Some of the people Down East don't agree. When it comes to scenery, Down East has some of the best, but as they say down there— you can't eat the scenery. When it comes to economic activity it's a pretty quiet place.

In Milbridge, a merchant said business is so bad, even the people who don't pay have stopped buying.

A Calais heavy equipment salesman was heard to say: "On Monday I sold a $20,000 front-end loader; on Tuesday I didn't sell a thing; and on Wednesday the fella who bought the front-end loader on Monday came back for a full refund. So you might say Tuesday's been my best day all week."

Trailer zone

They used to ask: What do Florida hurricanes and Maine divorces have in common?

The answer: In both cases some poor fella's going to lose his trailer.

Maine's Trailer zone is hard to pinpoint, but you'll know it when you see it. Just look around and you'll see what I mean.

Our state has always been home to a good number of folks who like to have wheels underneath them at all times—whether they're in a pickup or on a John Deere tractor. This love of mobility may have to do with our seafaring history when so many Mainers lived on sailing vessels and spent a good part of their lives traveling the world.

These days many Mainers feel that a trailer means freedom of movement. If your well goes dry, just move your trailer to a slab with a better well; if neighbors get too close, drag your trailer farther into the country.

Trailers and all that goes with them are as much a part of Maine as moose, lobsters, and lighthouses.

Trailers are also critical to the lawn ornament industry. It has been proven statistically that a 15 percent drop in trailer sales would create such a glut of Styrofoam geese, wooden puffins with windmill wings, and fake wooden wishing wells, that the whole businesses would be forced to shut down.

End zone

They tell the story about the fella from Massachusetts who wanted to avoid arrest so he fled to what he thought was the wilds of Maine. He was arrested in less than an hour.

What happened was he looked at a map of Maine and saw a wilderness with hardly any roads. He thought no one would ever find him in the Maine woods. He thought wrong.

In parts of Maine you can hear a car coming for miles. If you live on a road that only gets about three cars a week, it can be darned exciting when a car goes by, so you make sure you're at the window to see who it is coming down your road. In almost all cases, you'll know who it is and why they're driving by your house.

So, when the Massachusetts fella drove down the Sprague Falls Road in the End zone of Maine someone heard him coming, made sure they were at the window to see who it was, and then wondered why a strange car was headed down to the falls at this time of day.

A call to the dispatcher at the sheriff's office eventually brought a deputy down to check it out. After running the fella's license and registration, the deputy made the arrest without incident.

The point is, you may be at the end of the road here in Maine, but that doesn't mean that there's no one paying attention.

Flora and Fauna

Ask people Down East about Flora and Fauna and they'll think you're asking about the two "dancers" who worked the tent at the Blue Hill Fair for years. Nice girls. But no, when we mention flora and fauna, we're talking about our plants and animals and birds.

Evergreen trees

Since Maine's nickname is "The Pine Tree State," it doesn't take a so-called academic to tell you that the most important and famous tree in the state is the majestic white pine (*Pinus bigus money*). This tree—like many Mainers—prefers sunlight to shadow. The great white pine dominated the landscape and the economy of Maine throughout the 1800s, helping lumber barons amass fortunes, giving birth to the legend of Paul Bunyan, and helping Bangor emerge as the Lumber Capital of the World.

Of course, that ended after we cut all the white pine down. Thus, the Great White Pine Era gave way to the cute Christmas Tree Years.

We also have the red spruce (*Aintus a pinus*) which can grow as tall as 110 feet. After we cut down all the white pine we went after the red spruce to use for pulp. In a nod to diversity, our forests also have plenty of white spruce (*Aintus a pinus eitherus*) with silvery-brown bark and bluish-green needles.

You'll probably smell one of our balsam firs (*Xmasus treeus*) before you see it. Even if you don't know what it's called, you'll enjoy its fragrance, which makes this tree a popular choice for Christmas trees. It has flat needles that you'll find in your rug long after Christmas has passed, dark-purplish cones, and strings of popcorn.

Leaf trees

To Wabanaki tribes of yore, no tree was more useful than the paper birch (*Still notus pinus*). Indians used the birch's tough, white bark to craft baskets, canoes, and wigwams. The paper birch later gave way to the sturdier Fiberglass Tree (*Strongerus fibrus glassus*) as the key source for canoe materials.

The sugar maple (*Sweet stickius treeus*) was also important to Wabanakis and settlers alike because of its sweet sap that—when boiled for a few days—produces maple syrup.

Most of Maine's trees are pretty laid-back, but we do have the quaking aspen (*Nervosis treeus*), which got its name from the fact that the mildest breeze will set its leaves trembling something awful.

All three of these leafy or deciduous trees do their part to create the colors of our foliage season here in Maine, colors that make leaf peepers drive hundreds of miles (right past the *much duller* colors to be found in Vermont and New Hampshire) to get a look. Birch and aspen leaves turn yellow and maples turn a bright red or orange—colors made all the more striking by Maine's ever-present backdrop of dark evergreens.

Of course, culturally, the great apple tree (*Oldendaysus happy hourus*) has always been critical to Maine because it provides hard cider. In response to the popularity of Maine's hard cider, the geniuses in New Hampshire opened a gigantic drive-through liquor store *right on the highway* that, unless I am mistaken, gives away free booze to anyone older than ten. It was this mindset that gave rise to the saying on all New Hampshire license plates: LIVE FREE OR DIE DRUNK.

Poison oak, poison ivy and poison sumac

If you see something in the woods of Maine that's leafy and green, there is a chance that it's poison ivy, poison oak, or poison sumac and should be avoided. If you get a rash, well, like the song says, it's gonna take an ocean of calamine lotion. They say only 1 nanogram (a billionth of a gram) of the poison urushiol is needed to cause that ugly rash we're all familiar with. They also say that 500 people could itch from the amount of poison covering the head of a pin.

Who are the people saying these things? I don't have a clue. I just wish they'd stop talking and start doing something about finding a cure for the rash. Until they do, like I said, avoid leafy green plants.

Animals and Sea Creatures

Some people (tourism experts, mostly) might tell you there are really only two important animals in Maine: the moose and the lobster (hey, sounds like a good name for a book!). They are partly right, but Maine does have a diversity of wildlife.

Lobsters

The king of the sea is the lobster (*Makeus lotsa moneyus*).

Lobsters. Lobsters. Lobsters. Make that Maine Lobsters™ and get it right. Selling any lobster caught in an inferior state and calling it a Maine lobster is punishable by repeated dipping in a Maine lake in March. The Maine lobster is basically the reason why the Maine coast still exists. Without the lobster (and the industry it supports), the entire coastline would be cut off by huge summer cottages and resorts or preserved in a "natural state" as a playground for do-gooders from Cambridge.

Lobsters represent one of the great marketing success stories of all time. In the 1800s, *no one* ate lobster. It was ground up for fertilizer or used as chum to attract the more important mackerel. But there were just so many! So, the forebears of today's tourism professionals got together and said, "What can we do to get rid of at least some of these annoying, ugly creatures that are almost impossible to eat and mostly don't taste that good anyway?" They devised a plan. They invented melted butter and the lobster bib and convinced people that lobsters were a delicacy! We've been unloading them by the millions at exorbitant prices to tourists ever since. Genius.

But the lobster is not the only reason tourists come to Maine.

People also love crabs, clams, fish, scallops, butter, cole slaw and all sorts of other complementary food items (see Maine Cuisine).

Harbor seals

The harbor seal (*Cutus asa kittenus*) is a favorite with tourists. Five to six feet in length, with gray-brown fur, these marine mammals are easily spotted in, you guessed it—Maine's harbors. You'll also see them most anywhere along the coast or sunbathing on offshore ledges and islands.

These cute creatures like to wolf down herring, mackerel, fried clams with tartar sauce, and Big Macs to the tune of maybe 40 pounds a day, so they're not too popular among some fishermen.

Whales

The whale (*Lottsa blubberus*) is also a beloved creature around here, but also perhaps the dumbest animal on the entire planet. If a whale is swimming along and spots entangling and deadly fishing gear or the giant, spinning, Ginsu-sharp propeller of a ship, rather than take some type of evasive action, it swims right for them. I often wonder why Ahab went searching for the Great White Whale instead of just sitting around waiting for it to commit suicide.

Seagulls

The seagull (*Poopingus pestus*) is also known as gray-backed gull, black-backed Arctic gull, or stinkin' sea rat, and they often are called other names when they make a deposit on someone's head, steal a fisherman's bait, or rip off your toddler's Pop Tart. If you're at the beach, hold on to your hot dog. Gulls will swoop down and pinch the whole thing just as you're about to take a bite.

A middle-aged couple from Ohio was watching a flock of gulls on a dock in Bass Harbor when one of the gulls made a deposit on the husband's head. His wife said, "Just a minute, dear. I'll get some toilet paper." A fisherman standing nearby replied, "Wouldn't waste my time, deah. By the time you get back, that gull's gonna be halfway across the harbor."

Barnacles

The sea also has its share of annoying creatures. Coating the rocks along the shore at low water, you'll find a white layer of acorn barnacles (*Ouchus ouchus*).

These small crustaceans float to shore where they attach themselves to rocks, boat bottoms, and wharf pilings and form a tough shell that can be as annoying as a New York accent and sure do a number on your bare feet.

Puffins

The Atlantic puffin (*Notus a penguinus*) has become a very popular bird in recent years. That's not to say they haven't always been popular. Years ago ladies coveted these funny-looking birds' feathers for their fancy hats, and the puffins were hunted so much their numbers were in serious decline. But lo and behold, some bird lover came to the rescue, and now there are a number of restored and thriving puffin colonies.

You'll be hard-pressed to see a puffin while you're here, though, for two reasons. One is that they're much smaller than you'd think from looking at their pictures, and the second is that you have to make a special trip by boat out to one of the big rocks they nest on offshore. But to make up for that inconvenience, Maine stores offer lots of puffin paraphernalia, such as carvings, stuffed puffins (toys!) and T-shirts.

Moose

Not to be outdone by the coast, Maine's inland woods and lakes are filled with wildlife. And the most important is the moose (*Bigus doofus*). Legend claims that the inland tourist big-wigs were a little miffed at all the attention the coast and the lobster received. They set out to combat the imbalance. The trick was finding a dumb, gangly-looking animal that could rival the absurd look of the lobster. Cute, cuddly, or majestic animals need not apply. The winner after a nationwide search? The moose. But to be honest, they are big.

The good news is that moose have become very plentiful. The bad news, for the moose anyway, is that Maine has Moose Hunting Season every October. I have no scientific proof of this, but I believe hitting a moose when hunting is only slightly more difficult than hitting water when you fall out of a boat.

Black bears

Yup, we've got 'em. And not just the ones up in Orono, either. We're talking genuine black bears (*Runus awayus*).

I once asked Uncle Abner if he'd ever run into any bears in all his years in Maine. Of course he had.

"I was out picking blueberries on a hot August day when I came to the end of a patch and looked up, and there staring me dead in the eye was a three-hundred-pound black bear just sitting there picking his own berries."

"What did you do, Uncle?" I asked.

"I dropped my berries and got up and ran."

"What'd the bear do?"

"He dropped his berries and got up and chased me. And the more I ran, the more he chased me. I'd scamper up a tree and he—of course—would scamper right up behind me. I'd climb down the other side and he was right there. Running up steep hills didn't slow him down at all. He kept running right behind me.

"Finally, I ran out onto a frozen pond and he was afraid to follow me. He finally got tired of waiting and ambled off into the woods."

"Wait a minute," I said. "A frozen pond?"

"Ayuh, that's right," said Uncle Abner.

"But you said you were picking blueberries in August."
"That's a fact," said Uncle Abner. "But that friggin' bear chased me all the way to Christmas!"

White-tailed deer

The white-tailed deer (*Dontus shootus Ima Bambius*) is popular with nature lovers and meat lovers. Hunting is a big part of Maine's culture. Deer season is used by many Maine residents to get time off in the fall so they can recover from tourist season, and it's used by others to delineate the end of the summer season, aka, the working season, and winter, aka, the unemployment check season.

Some visitors (and wacky protesters) actually think that the goal of deer hunters is to kill a deer for their freezer. That was true in the olden days, but fact is, today many hunters don't care to bag a deer at all—they just want to go up to camp to drink beer, not bathe, and look sharp in blaze orange and camouflage. Actually bagging a deer would only ruin the plan. Once shot, a deer has to be dressed out, hauled out of the woods, loaded into your pickup, taken to a tagging station, driven home, skinned, butchered, wrapped, and frozen. That is all a mite bit tougher than going to the McDonald's drive-through and ordering a Quarter Pounder Value Meal. You might as well stay at work if you're gonna go through all that aggravation.

Blackflies

The old saying goes: Blackflies don't bite, they suck. Truer words were never spoken. Still, the blackfly (*Bugus ruinus campingus*) could be in the running as the official state bird or state animal. There is even a breeders association. Really.

Maine History Timeline

17,000 BC   Last glacier begins to recede. Ice machines soon appear.

11,000 BC   Maine is free of the glacier, except for a few ice caps in northern regions, which still exist in parts of Fort Kent and Madawaska.

7500–6000 BC   Sea levels rise and Atlantic Ocean reaches present-day Millinocket. Prices of houses that suddenly have ocean frontage skyrocket. Speculators over-build waterfront condos and market collapses as sea pulls away.

1497–1499   John and Sebastian Cabot explore coast of Maine, establishing English claims and open first clam shacks. Heated arguments erupt over fried clams with batter versus crumbs.

1524   Giovanni da Verrazano explores coast for French, is mooned by Maine Indians and names Maine "The Land of the Bad People." State tourism officials are not amused.

1604   Samuel de Champlain sights and names Mount Desert Island. Rich rusticators whine that sighting opens door for common folk and other riffraff to invade their Eden. Invent secluded Northeast Harbor in response.

1607–1608   Popham Colony settled in 1607 at mouth of Kennebec River. In 1608, George Popham dies, Raleigh Gilbert returns to England, and colony is abandoned, but not before first North American–built ship, *Virginia*, is constructed.

1622	Sir Fernando Gorges and John Mason are granted all lands between Merrimac River and Kennebec River, establishing Province of Maine. They invent slogan, "Maine—the way life should be."
1628	Trading post opened by Plymouth Colony at present-day site of Augusta. Residents include Captain Miles Standish. Sales of fudge and salt-water taffy support colony. Fried dough soon invented.
1636	Maine's first court convenes at Saco in response to speed traps on I-95.
1647	Kittery, first town in Maine, established. Locals complain only jobs available are service jobs at shopping outlets.
1750	Maine population hits 10,000. *Portland Press Herald* runs 109-part series decrying that sprawl is now destroying Maine.
1763	Treaty of Paris ends French and Indian Wars, officially ending French claims on North America.
1774	Ogunquit businessmen make first attempt at banning any business that might be actual competition.
1775	First naval battle of Revolutionary War is fought in Machias Bay. Forty colonists capture English warship *Margaretta*. Massachusetts historians quickly claim they didn't see it so it doesn't count.
1775	In eventful year, British burn Falmouth (now Portland), but fortunately the Marden family buys damaged goods as salvage and opens first of their popular chain of discount stores.

1779	British forces occupy Castine, take control of Eastern Maine.
1790	George Washington orders Portland Head Light built, effectively reenergizing calendar, postcard and key chain market.
1794	Bowdoin College, Maine's first college, established, beginning steady flow of rich, spoiled trust fund kids into Maine.
1800	Maine's population reaches 150,000. *Press Herald* runs follow-up 206-part series saying we told you before, but now sprawl is really, really bad.
1812	British attack Maine, occupy coast during War of 1812.
1820	Maine granted divorce from Massachusetts and enters Union as the twenty-third state. Residents of Boston immediately begin making plans for campaign to turn Maine into wilderness national park. According to their analysis, kicking everyone out but moose will generate millions of dollars in economic development.
1824	Maine State Prison built in Thomaston. NO VACANCY sign soon goes up.
1838	Bloodless Aroostook War regarding boundary dispute between Maine and Canada begins and ends. The line is decided officially by Webster-Ashburton Treaty in 1842.
1851	With the Maine Law (Prohibition), state outlaws manufacture or sale of liquor. New Hampshire responds by opening liquor stores at all Maine–New Hampshire crossings.
1861–1865	Nearly 73,000 men from Maine fight for Union in Civil War.

1866	Great Fire razes much of Portland. Marden's expands.
1875	First lobster pound established in Vinalhaven. Melted butter and Wet Nap industries explode.
1884	Bath Iron Works established. Workers strike next day.
1898	Battleship USS *Maine* blown up in Havana Harbor.
1912	L.L. Bean opens shop in Freeport. Some people claim this is when Maine was actually founded, at least so's anyone would notice.
1919	Lafayette National Park (renamed Acadia National Park in 1928) established on Mount Desert Island. Ellsworth (Wabanaki for "Get fuel and use the restroom before reaching someplace actually scenic") gloms on and dubs itself "Crossroads of Down East Maine."
1947	First Maine Lobster Festival held in Rockland. Number of Maine artists and pickle makers immediately triples.
1947	Maine Turnpike opened from Kittery to Portland. State promises tolls won't be in place long.
1947	Bar Harbor largely destroyed by fire. Marden's expands yet again.
1955	Turnpike extended to Augusta. Residents elsewhere ask why.
1975	Last river log drive in Maine.
1970s	Back to Land movement brings many transplants to state. Showers taken per capita drops dramatically.
2002	John McDonald writes *A Moose and a Lobster Walk into a Bar*.

Discovery and Colonization of Maine

At least 500 years before Columbus discovered America for Spain, Leif Ericson and a crew of Viking sailors are thought to have explored the Maine coast and may have landed and tried to settle down here. Trouble is, it was summer and seasonal prices were ridiculous. It's thought, given a very low per diem, that they were so discouraged by the cost of meals and lodging they returned to Scandinavia to become sweater makers. They never return.

Around 1498, John Cabot—an Italian sailor in the employ of King Henry VII of England—may have explored the Maine coast. There's no concrete evidence of his visit because he didn't call anyone while here, so there are no phone records, nor did he send any postcards. His descendants eventually ended up in Vermont where they bought some cows and started making wicked good cheese.

A century after Cabot's voyage, we think a number of European ships came by for brief visits to this area, but we're not positive. We also think some of them came ashore to repair their hulls and rigging and to dry fish but, again, we're not sure. All we know is that if they were here, they didn't talk to any locals. Sort of like early versions of the rich folks at Northeast Harbor.

First colony

In the middle of August in 1607—without reservations at the height of tourist season, no less—a small group of hardy souls landed at the mouth of the mighty Kennebec (then known as the almost-but-not-quite mighty Sagadahoc) River aboard two sturdy ships, *Mary and John* and *Gift of God*.

The proprietors of this proposed colony hoped to make all kinds of money catching fish, cutting lumber, trading for furs, digging for minerals, selling fried dough, and gathering all kinds of valuable medicinal herbs.

After coming ashore and having a nice picnic, the new colonists got right down to business and designated a "swimsuit optional" section of Popham Beach. Since nearby motels and B&Bs were filled, the colonists then built dwellings, a storehouse, and a church.

Some of the Popham settlers also began building a 30-ton pinnace (PIN-iss)—a small schooner-rigged vessel named *Virginia*. It was the first ship built in North America and was a harbinger of the future—shipbuilding on the Kennebec.

According to Robert C. Tristram Coffin, the first Protestant church service in Maine was conducted in Popham Colony by Anglican clergyman Richard Seymour. At the service, we believe, he also announced the first Vegas Night and Bean Supper.

Unfortunately, after a few months of relative harmony, things in the colony started to go downhill fast. Even though Portland's rowdy Old Port bars were still a few centuries away, the men of Popham managed to get into fistfights and drunken brawls, we suspect over ambiguous boundary lines and skeeball. All kinds of bitter quarrels arose among the colonists, and eventually almost half the men were shipped back to England for "conduct unbecoming even a felon." After the brutal Maine winter of 1607–08 the rest threw up their hands and skedaddled for Florida, where they bought condos and invented shuffleboard.

Colonial era (sort of)

Maine got caught up in the many battles of the French and Indian Wars that pitted France against Great Britain for control of America. The wars started in 1675 with King Philip's War and ended in 1763 with the Seven Years' War. The various wars caused much bloodshed and hard feelings. Some Maine towns nearly depopulated for fear of attack and others because of attack, including the York Massacre, which also destroyed most of the town's precolonial buildings. The Treaty of Paris in 1763 brought the French and Indian Wars to an end, and also put an end to all French claims in North America.

After the wars, the population of Maine took off like a house afire, but not without encouragement from Massachusetts, which created *Down East* magazine to sell overpriced lots and houses to anyone who would settle in what they called their "northern province." Many of the lots were advertised with water views and "lots of potential" to gloss over the brutal winters, isolation, and lack of cable TV.

As the population grew, Mainers became frustrated with what they considered unfair colonial tax policies of the British Parliament. Considered most onerous was the tax on coffee brandy and milk, the preferred drink of Maine since the beginning of time.

A year after the famous Boston Tea Party of 1773, Maine staged its own version when a group of men burned a shipment of scratch tickets stored at a York 7-Eleven. Didn't that make them Brits some ugly, I tell you.

Finally, when open warfare erupted at Lexington and Concord, hundreds of Maine men volunteered to join the struggle for independence. And not just so they could head south in the winter, but because their mothers told them the army had a good pension and they could retire after twenty years.

Maine played an important role in Revolutionary War history with many battles and events taking place right here in the Pine Tree State (you might not have heard of them because Massachusetts thinks it *owns* Revolutionary history and strictly adheres to the policy: "If it didn't happen here, it didn't happen).

In 1775 British warships under the command of the notorious and obnoxious Captain Henry Mowatt shelled and burned Falmouth (now Portland). It was an act intended to punish residents because the local clam shacks refused to the use the English term "chips" when referring to French fries, and the King hated anything French. As you might expect, the people of Falmouth were none too happy about the shelling, and it only served to stiffen their opposition to British

The first naval battle of the Revolution occurred in June of 1775 when a group of Maine patriots captured the armed British cutter *Margaretta* off Machias.

rule. In a famous speech, Hezekiah Wills declared, "It is my God-given right to own a gun, not wear a seat belt, and to eat French fries—*not* the King's so-called chips."

One of Mowatt's cannonballs hit the Unitarian Church on Congress Street and was lodged in a wall. Mainers, being frugal, made it into a chandelier when the church was later remodeled. You can see it there today.

Later that year, many Maine men went along with Colonel Benedict Arnold on his long march through the North Woods in a courageous, but fruitless attempt to capture the walled city of Quebec. No one knows exactly what happened. Some of their wives claim Benedict and the boys got lost right from the start, but still could have made it if they would have just stopped and asked the natives for directions.

Maine statehood

Following the Revolution, Mainers began expressing their annoyance at being ruled from Boston and pressed for secession from the pretentiously named Commonwealth of Massachusetts. In yet another famous speech, Hezekiah Wills uttered the famous rallying cry: "Jumpin' Jesus, and we thought the Brits were bad!"

At first, prosperous coastal clammers and wormers resisted the separation movement. But after the War of 1812—during which the British took over and controlled much of the Maine coast while the "protectors" in Boston were either drunk or stuck in traffic—it became obvious to anyone paying attention that Massachusetts couldn't or didn't want to provide adequate protection for Mainers.

While British occupation was the catalyst, popular sentiment became unanimous behind the idea of statehood after Massachusetts demanded the state install a Transpass toll collection system on the highway. Eventually Congress established Maine as the twenty-third state as part of the Missouri Compromise of 1820.

By this time the population of Maine had reached nearly 300,000, spread across nine counties and 236 towns.

Initially, political leaders chose Portland as the state capital, but real Mainers quickly put an end to that foolishness. In fact, it is often said the only thing early Mainers could agree on was that the state capital should be *anywhere* but Portland. So, in 1832 all the state's important papers were packed up in a couple of Hannaford bags and hauled to Augusta, which is a

Wabanaki word meaning "small town with lots of strip malls."
After finally seeing Augusta, the powers that be were not overly
impressed, but again the popular sentiment was summed up
thusly: "Well, at least it ain't friggin' Portland."

The Northeast boundary dispute, or the Canadians get testy

Just like our private property lines here in Maine, the precise
boundary between Maine and New Brunswick remained a matter of conjecture that occasionally erupted into heated arguments. The treaty that ended the Revolutionary War was
supposed to fix the borderline, but for some reason no one knew
exactly where it was. When asked the exact location of the border, Mainers would point toward the north and say "over there
in those woods." Meanwhile, the folks in New Brunswick
would point toward the south and say, "Over in those woods.
Pass me another Labatts."

Eventually the name-calling and disputes grew worse and
threatened to become a full-fledged shooting match. The Maine
Legislature certainly didn't want to get outmaneuvered or out-
fought by Canada, for crying out loud, so it raised funds to support a military force of 10,000 men to protect the state's border
claims at Madawaska. (Incidentally, it is believed this was the
last Maine Legislature to even have a clue where Madawaska is
located.)

Several hundred British regulars were dispatched to the
scene from Quebec. So, then Washington, D.C., got involved
and approved $10 million for military expenses if war broke
out. It was getting some ugly.

Ultimately, nearly 50,000 troops were massed and readied
for action, and Major General Winfield Scott was dispatched to

the scene. Scott managed to work out a temporary agreement between the two parties before the Aroostook War reached the point of bloodshed.

In a key meeting over coffee and crullers at a Dunkin' Donuts, both sides presented their arguments. Each argument was considered (although Canada's argument was actually discounted 30 percent), and the Webster-Ashburton Treaty officially settled the question of where Maine's northeast boundary lay—over in the river somewhere.

The Maine law

The world's first Total Abstinence Society was founded in Portland in 1815. By 1851 Maine's teetotalers developed enough political clout to force the enactment of a state law prohibiting the sale of alcoholic spirits except for "medicinal and mechanical" purposes. The law increased the need for alcohol-based medicines by a million percent. The so-called "Maine Law" remained in effect in one form or another until the repeal of National Prohibition in 1934.

Civil War

Maine entered the Union as a free state and with a strong anti-slavery tradition. Abolitionist societies were active throughout the state years before the outbreak of the Civil War. It's also worth mentioning that author Harriet Beecher Stowe, the author of *Uncle Tom's Cabin,* was the wife a Bowdoin College professor and spent years living and writing in Brunswick.

Some 73,000 Maine men served with the Union forces and over 7,000 of them lost their lives during the conflict.

Maine contributed two great Union generals—Oliver Otis Howard, who performed brilliantly at Gettysburg and Bull Run, and Joshua Lawrence Chamberlain, the hero of Gettysburg's Little Round Top. Chamberlain also commanded the Union troops to whom Lee surrendered at Appomattox. After the war he was elected governor of Maine.

Modern history

Not much has really happened since the end of the nineteenth century. In brief, log drives ended, the paper industry declined, offshore fishing dried up, and lobster fishing exploded. Out-of-staters bought up most of the good land. Wooden shacks were replaced by double-wide trailers. Everyone started to work at Wal-Mart. The Boston Red Sox won the 2004 World Series. And, of course, tourism got really, *really huge.*

Maine Basics

What do you pack when you're planning a visit to Maine? Cash and credit cards, period.

We prefer that you bring almost *nothing* with you to Maine, and while you're here buy everything you need and lots of stuff that you don't. We spend a lot of time in the winter thinking up things to sell to tourists, and come spring we mortgage the trailer, the snowmobile, the pickup, the dog, the cat, and anything else we can find to get enough money to buy things to sell. We fully expect you folks to snap up all our stuff and cram it into your vehicles and haul it to hell out of here.

Not only is this process good for the state's economy, but it is also critical to our entire trash-removal infrastructure. Our system is predicated on tourists loading their cars with trinkets and perceived treasures and hauling them across state lines. If this doesn't happen, our dumps and backyards soon will be overwhelmed, leaving no room for more important items such as broken-down refrigerators and junk cars. It would be akin to an environmental disaster.

Tips for Tourists

1. The more fishing nets, wooden traps, barnacle-covered buoys, and other flotsam and jetsam hanging outside a Down East establishment, the less genuine the enterprise will be inside.
2. When you discover an ideal spot while vacationing in Maine, don't be a knucklehead and tell all your friends about it as soon as you return home.
3. Don't sit at a table in the middle of a local restaurant and talk real loud about how cheap everything is here. We can arrange to charge you more if you like.
4. Don't ask someone if they were the inspiration for a Stephen King novel. They probably don't like to talk about it.
5. There *are* such things as dumb questions. Keep them to yourself.
6. Do drive safely on our roads; don't drive on things like our fancy lawns. Years ago most Maine homes didn't have lawns. You could drive your car right into someone's dooryard and park wherever. Some of Maine's homeowners still observe this tradition and have large, mostly level yards of mostly gravel where a lawn might be expected. Elsewhere around the main house—in keeping with the old ways—they'll also have a tasteful mix of weeds, puckerbrush, dead flowers, and a few neatly arranged stored items like cinder blocks, tripods, engine blocks, appliances, car, truck and snowmobile parts, sinks and—of course—a few satellite dishes.
7. Do enjoy our way of speaking; don't try it yourself.
8. Do stop and ask folks for directions; don't take those directions too seriously.
9. Do ask what people in a town do for excitement; don't laugh at the answer.
10. Don't complain about the weather.

How to dress

Mainers are pretty laid-back about how to dress and what to wear. In some places sweatpants and steel-toed work boots are appropriate to wear even at your finer restaurants, and are always appropriate for an outing to buy scratch tickets. Reindeer-patterned sweaters and plaid flannel shirts can be worn year-round, and flowered muumuus (clothing for full-figured women) are as common as socks, and not just in the mornings. Budweiser and John Deere hats often can be worn at social events without offense, and it would be a sacrilege to criticize any garment or piece of clothing that is seen as a tribute to Dale Earnhardt Sr. under any circumstance.

Of course—and this is critical—just because something is okay for the natives does not automatically make it okay for tourists.

So, here are a few tips.

Packing necessities

Sunscreen	Well, we can dream.
Sunglasses	See above.
Bug spray	Important, above all else. Buy in the special oil-drum size, if possible.
More bug spray	If you run out, you will—and I mean this—be eaten alive and not make it back home.
Rain gear	Forget it and you have doomed yourself to endless fog and ceaseless rain.
Blaze orange	You may not like it, but in the fall (i.e., hunting season) it is all the rage for those who wish to actually survive the vacation.

One day a team of state surveyors was out working in western Oxford County. After spending an entire day going through swamps and fields and puckerbrush, they realized that a farm located on the border was not in Maine at all, but was actually in New Hampshire.

One surveyor was given the task of breaking the news to the owner. That surveyor fella was a little concerned; he didn't know how the farm's owner would take to being told his farm had just moved from Maine to New Hampshire, of all places. He walked up to the farmhouse, and found the owner harvesting some pumpkins.

"Sir," he said to the old man, "I'm with the state and we are trying to straighten out all the borderlines around here, and I have some bad news. After surveying your farm, we have discovered that your place isn't in Maine at all—it's actually in New Hampshire."

The old man looked a mite shaken at first, but then a smile spread across his face. "Well, thank you, young fella, and thank the good Lord, too. Truth be told, I was just wondering how Mother and I were possibly going to make it through another Maine winter."

Fashion tips

Make sure your behind is fully covered. In addition to simple modesty, our blackflies and mosquitos can make quite a meal out of an exposed southern end.

Wear a hat to the beach. Seagulls are always circling overhead; need I say more?

Wear clothing with deep pockets, the better to fill with your credit cards and cash.

Wear sensible shoes, even in our cities. Stilettos may look nice, but they don't do well with our brick sidewalks, cobblestone streets or beaches. Any footwear sold by L.L. Bean will suffice.

Don't wear those cute moose antler hats and go for a walk in the woods.

Don't wear much, if any, perfume. It tolls the blackflies and mosquitos something wicked, especially really hungry ones.

Wearing lobster hats (you know, the ones with claws on top) will ensure a snicker, and mark you as not only a tourist, but a goofy one at that, who will be charged a significantly higher price on anything possible.

If you like to wear a baseball cap that doesn't have a Red Sox logo on it, please respectfully—and for your own personal safety—refrain from putting it on while you are within our borders. Let me be clear: We all *hate* the New York Yankees. We cannot be held responsible for actions taken to remove offending headgear from perpetrators.

Do not slip into a Speedo if you are of the male gender. If you must—and we certainly can't think of any good reasons why you must—please limit this action to Old Orchard Beach, where there is a 30-foot section reserved for this fashion faux pas. Female sunbathers, however, should feel free to wear a thong. (Well, some of them, anyway.)

Do not go overboard with jewelry if you are, again, of the male gender. Wedding rings and watches are okay, but that's about it. Neck chains, tongue (are you people nuts?) rings, eyebrow rings, and other such bling are more appropriate for say, Cape Cod.

Gilligan hats may seem like a good idea, but . . .

Flannel shirts are a good all-round product and can be worn even in August.

Hip boots are for real fishermen only, please.

No Hawaiian shirts or cruise wear. Do you see any palm trees around here, chummy?

One hot summer day, Tewkey Butler decided he would take a train ride to Albany to visit his Aunt Ella.

Once on board he found a seat and sat there minding his own business. Soon a conductor came along and yelled, "You can't leave your bag in the aisle! You've got to stow it above," as he headed toward the back of the train.

Tewkey didn't say anything; he just sat there.

A few minutes later the same conductor was back and again he yelled, "You can't leave your bag in the aisle! It's got to be stowed above."

Tewkey nodded, but didn't say a word.

Fifteen minutes later the conductor came back through and sees the bag still sitting right there in the middle of the aisle. By this time he is some ugly. He picks up the bag, goes to the door and heaves the bag out into the puckerbrush. The bag broke open as it hit the ground, spreading clothes along the side of the tracks. It was some mess.

The conductor comes back to Tewkey's seat and says, "There, what do you think of that?"

"Well, I wouldn't think much," Tewkey said, "if it were my bag."

Tipping

Maine doesn't have many places that feature what's known in cities elsewhere as valet parking. That's because Mainers figure, why give some stranger the keys to your pickup so they can drive it to some undisclosed location and then demand a hefty tip for bringing it back.

But we do have lots of honest, hardworking people in the tourist industry who deserve a decent tip for serving your food and cleaning up your hotel room. And I don't want to give away any secrets, but we do have ways of dealing with those who avoid tipping. Just remember: Your waitress spends a lot of alone time with your food, and she probably has a boyfriend who needs to pay the cable bill. We suggest a tip of 50 percent; 75 percent if you drive a foreign car that will take a long time to repair.

Smoking

Years ago most everyone in Maine smoked and smoked a lot. Kids often started smoking at eleven or twelve and puffed away until they passed away, usually of some smoking-related condition. I remember going to a bingo hall or bean supper and the smoke was so thick you couldn't see across the table. Not anymore.

These days they may as well put a NO SMOKING sign on the Piscataqua Bridge coming into Maine, because you'll get in trouble—or at least some wicked nasty looks—smoking in just about any public place. **Tip:** If you really need to smoke, find the doorway of an office building and smoke with the sad-looking group huddled up and puffing during their break.

Types of Roads

Because most of our ancestors arrived in boats and early settlers continued to use boats to get around from one place to another, not much time was spent fussing with what we now call "roads." Honoring that tradition, our modern-day road crews don't spend much time "working" on our roads, either.

Our road guys basically figure that if people like you don't like riding on roads bumpy enough to shake the gold fillings clean out of your laser-whitened teeth, you can go home. If you're going to risk it, here's a general description of what to consider when choosing a road.

Route 1

The gift-shop capital of the world and one of the slowest roads in America. Always crowded and always under construction. Opens up considerably east of Bangor.

Tote road

A tote road is a private road cut through the woods in order to "tote"—get it?—something out of the woods, mostly pulpwood. Tote roads are also used for toting bagged game like deer and moose during hunting season. These days some tote roads are incorporated into Maine's vast network of well-groomed snowmobile trails. If you break down on a tote road, chances are you will never be heard from again.

Logging road

A tote road by another name is a logging road.

Country road

A country road is a road in the country (what are the chances?) that looks like it doesn't go anywhere. In fact, many roads don't.

Some country roads follow early Indian or settler paths along the coast or wend their way through the woods from one town to another and suddenly just end. Country roads are usually less

During World War II the government built an emergency landing strip in Cherryfield for B-17s and other big bombers that needed an emergency landing field after flying across the North Atlantic.

After the war the town's selectmen decided to make a commercial airfield out of the strip, because they were told that a town would never get anywhere in the modern world unless it had an airport. All modern tourists want the option of flying to a destination, they were told. So, the town manager was instructed to send out requests for proposals to all the big airlines—Delta, TWA, American—but not one responded.

About six months later selectmen received a reply from a little-known airline called Old Crow whose motto was: "Nothing scares us." The terse reply made it clear that the company was anxious to become part of the Cherryfield experience. Having no other takers the town fathers let them open a ticket window and begin regular service to various towns in and out of Maine.

The most immediate effect of the new service was a drop in betting on the trotters at the Cherryfield Fair that summer. Instead of betting $10 or $20 at the track, people were going to the Old Crow ticket window and saying: "I'd like to take a chance on Flight 24 to Presque Isle."

The airline tickets were a bit more expensive, but the game was a lot more sporting.

crowded than major highways and provide ample opportunities for you to stop and ask: "Where'n hell are we?"

Ridge road

Every Maine town with even the smallest hill will most likely have a ridge road, and the people living on it will most likely be called "ridge runners." Ridge roads also lend their names to halls and churches, so you'll have a Ridge Road, Ridge Church and maybe a Ridge Runner Grange.

River road

If a town has a ridge then it'll most likely have a valley. Running through that valley—more than likely—will be a river. Are you following me?

Running up along one bank and down along the other of most rivers are roads. I guarantee one of those roads will be called River Road, but I can't tell you from here which one. That's up to someone else. I don't know who, but I do know that the responsibility of making such decisions is far above my pay grade.

Town road

These roads are maintained by the town (meaning local tax-payers) and continually argued about at Town Meeting. **Warning**: The potholes in town roads have been known to grow so large as to swallow up Volvos whole and then come up to get a Toyota for dessert. Consider driving a big hunk of Detroit iron or avoid these roads whenever possible.

State road

Where the town road ends, the state road begins, until it hits another town, and so forth and so on.

Professional traffic sports

Those who enjoy traffic sports will be interested to learn that last year we saw one of the most active and competitive seasons ever in the highly popular and rapidly growing Motor Home Division. Motor homes, of course, have become known as the dangerous fat globules in Maine's once cholesterol-free traffic arteries.

Basically, it's like this. Friendly motor-home owners compete to see who can acquire the longest, widest, highest, and slowest motor home on the planet. Serious competitors know it's not enough just to buy a 30-foot or 40-foot monster and get out there on the road. No sir-ree, these dedicated drivers like to attach a full-size car to the back of their motor homes and then, just for good measure, pile on bikes, lawn chairs, satellite dishes, canoes, grills, and John Deere tractors.

The whole idea of the sport is to drive through a given state—like Maine—without ever going over, oh, say, 8 mph (even down a steep hill with a strong tailwind). You earn points for each car you collect behind you. The prime regions for this sport are those that feature the narrowest and most congested coastal roads in the state—such as the Boothbay Harbor and Bar Harbor regions, which are perennial favorites.

The current state record in the Motor Home Division was set on August 16, 2005, by Ken Spritzenmacher, a retired divorce lawyer from Vermillion, South Dakota. Mr. S. actually collected behind his motor home an impressive 13,867 vehicles filled with 58,391 hot, angry, frustrated drivers and passengers while driving on Route 3 between Ellsworth and Bar Harbor. Way to go, Kenny.

Getting Around

Maps

Call me nuts (others have), but I never use road maps when traveling and—if you really want to experience Maine—neither should you. A long time ago I decided that the best way to travel anywhere was in a map-free vehicle. That way when you come unexpectedly upon a road—or even a new town—it's a complete surprise; it's exciting. That babbling brook you almost drove straight into because you didn't know there was no bridge to cross it? Lovely, isn't it? That kind of touring is what I call adventurous. Those newfangled Global Positioning System gadgets are plainly for sissies.

The way I see it, the great explorers never used maps—at least not on their first voyage. They didn't have GPS, either, and they had some of the greatest adventures in recorded history. Following in the footsteps of the great explorers—that's me, that's what I like to do.

My Uncle Abner tells the story of a young couple from New York who got lost up north and stopped at the local country store to ask for directions. The man stepped out of his Volvo, walked into the store, and asked the storekeeper where the road to the left went.

"Mooselookmeguntic," the man answered.

"What if I take the road to the right?"

"Wittapitloc."

"Well, then," the man said, "what if I just keep going straight?"

"Mattawamqueag."

The man returned to the car and his wife asked, "Well, do you know where we are going now?"

"Hell, no," the man said. "The guy in there doesn't even speak English."

The famous French explorer Jacques Cartier set out on an adventure with no map to guide him and ended up discovering Canada. Way to go, Jacques!

When asked where he was off to, did Cartier say: "I'm thinking I'd like to go out and discover Canada?" Of course not. Did he have maps of Canada onboard to guide him? No, he did not. He just set off on a trip. And, not only did Cartier discover Canada, he is also credited with discovering the St. Lawrence River. Not bad for a guy out sailing around without a map.

I just know there is some undiscovered place in Aroostook County that I will stumble upon one day, lay claim to it, and plant the flag. Just think about it. A town in The County all to myself. On second thought, maybe I ought to get myself a map.

Detours

Travel Maine roads in the warm weather and you'll be detoured by road-repair crews about every ten miles, minimum.

You know you're approaching a road repair crew when you see a sign that says MEN WORKING. These fellas learned a long time ago that they needed to post that sign, because if they didn't tell you they were working you'd certainly never guess it to look at them. But it is no longer a comfortable life.

 We used to have passenger trains running up and down the state years ago. My friend Elmer Davis once had to make a trip to Boston. He walked into the train station in Bangor and asked the clerk for a round-trip ticket. When the snooty clerk snapped, "A round-trip ticket to *where*?" Elmer snapped right back: "I hope right back here!"

Last spring a lot of our road crews feared that they would be outsourced after an article appeared in the local paper under the headline: JAPANESE INVENT SHOVEL THAT LEANS ON ITSELF.

"That's it for us," crew members sighed. But fortunately for the fellas, as of today, the self-leaning shovel has not yet replaced too many of them.

Also, essential to any road-repair team are the two sign persons who stand all day on either end of the road repair holding signs that read STOP on one side and SLOW on the other. This is a complicated job. First, you must be able to distinguish—quick as a wink—between the words *Stop* and *Slow*. Sure, it sounds easy, but you try it sometime after standing in the hot sun breathing road dust for several hours as ill-tempered drivers go by expressing all kinds of slanderous opinions about you and your kin.

If you encounter these sign-holding persons during your visit, and you most certainly will, please be kind to them.

They're good folks with high aspirations, mostly. In their spare time, they're working on skills like shovel-leaning so they can get promoted someday.

Bottlenecks

Route 3 between Ellsworth and Bar Harbor has been designated—by some self-appointed band of freelance listmakers—as one of the worst bottlenecks in the country.

These so-called researchers said that the road connecting the mainland to Mount Desert Island is among the top twenty-five most congested tourist destinations in the nation. That classification left some local officials and summer visitors scratching their heads. (We're not suggesting that they wouldn't have been scratching their heads, anyway, or any other parts of their bodies, it being bug season, but this just gave them a good excuse to do such a thing in public.)

As expected, a Bar Harbor official expressed deep concern that the route's status on the list might scare some tourists away from that area. But an unexpected reaction to the bottleneck study came from officials in other Maine towns who wanted to know just why their local bottlenecks *didn't* make the cut.

Proving that any publicity is good publicity, a resident of Skowhegan said: "Have these list makers, these researchers, ever tried to get through downtown Skowhegan in summer when people are heading to camp or to the lake? It's chaos. I'm a little miffed we weren't mentioned and that the coast continues to get all the attention."

In Naples, a town official proclaimed that the Causeway—Western Maine's Manic Mile—was one of the worst bottlenecks that any group of traffic engineers ever devised. "Can you believe we only got Honorable Mention," she asked indignantly.

"Stupid coast." She issued a challenge to MDI to prove that it really was more congested than Naples and asked for unbiased officials, preferably from Bridgton, to judge.

Other town officials, however, didn't appear to be too perturbed by their town's absence on the list. They just used the bottleneck study as an excuse to uncork a bottle of their own.

Speed limits

Most distances and speed limits in Maine are shown in miles and miles per hour—as they should be and as we've always liked them. However, some signs give distances in kilometers. This is mostly for our Canadian neighbors whom we love like family, but like family we love it when these hockey players come for a brief visit and then leave, eh?

The speed limit on the Maine Turnpike is 65 mph but that—of course—is just a friendly suggestion. If you insist on poking along at that speed don't be surprised if every other SUV, car, truck, camper, motor home, trailer, bike, scooter, ATV, and farm tractor goes flying past.

We also encourage drivers—as a rule—to pass on the left. Passing on the right has been accomplished successfully on occasion, usually after BYOB night at the local Legion Hall, but the police generally frown on the practice.

Road signs

Road signs are mostly legible and even visible on most roads, but—just to have fun and break the monotony—some road signs are placed where there is no way you'll ever see them or are so perforated with buckshot they are illegible.

Mainers don't just give out information to tourists; we try to get a little information in return. Which brings to mind the time I was sitting on Dickey Merrill's front porch and a couple from Massachusetts stopped their Volvo and asked for directions to Bangor. Dickey, a direction-giver of world-class standing, started right off giving one direction after another. The wife, on the passenger side, wrote it all down. When Dickey was done, her window went up and off they went.

Fifteen minutes later, the same couple in the same car stopped in front of the house again.

You see, Dickey had directed them up one side of town, across the river, back down the other side of town, and back across the river again—a complete circle.

When the wife saw Dickey she realized what he'd done. She put her window down again and proceeded to give Dickey a tongue-lashing so severe I swear it started to blister the paint right off the front of his house. Dickey claims he hadn't heard such strong language since the last church social.

When the woman was done with her tirade, she demanded an apology. But Dickey, not a man to get flustered easily, was cool as a cucumber.

"Listen, deah," he said. "I just wanted to make sure you could follow directions before I wasted my time directing you all the way to Bangor."

To make matters worse, the state has banned billboards (meaning signs clearly legible from the highway) and replaced them with miniature blue signs that cannot be read until you are right on top of them. While you are trying to figure out what they say you have missed your turn or driven into the gutter.

The state of Maine tends to treat directional signs as if they were a precious resource, using as few as possible and usually, because of budget considerations, leaving out at least one critical sign that could easily direct a traveler to their desired destination. In all honesty, though, it is not all the state's fault. At one time, the DOT developed a plan that would create enough signs to properly direct people to where they wanted to go without getting lost and, get this, along the quickest route possible. Let me explain; a road sign system would be created that would get people from Point A to Point B, for example, in just thirty minutes, instead of the 437.5 hours it would take along the "business route." However, all the businesses that prey off people who are tired, lost, hungry, and desperate (that is, tourists) got some ugly and the plan was abandoned. We have no proof, but we understand those same forces are currently developing a plan to "direct" people trying to get from Kittery to Bar Harbor through Fort Kent to help all the struggling country stores along the way.

Traffic approaching from the left in a traffic circle has the right of way (although that could be just a rumor). After a traffic circle accident, a Down Easter once argued in court that he was on the auto equivalent of a starboard tack as he entered the circle and everyone knows that a sailing vessel on a starboard tack has an undisputed right of way. The flatlander judge was only mildly amused.

Pedestrian right-of-way

We're told there's a law that says drivers must stop for pedestrians in crosswalks, but don't take it too seriously—it could be dangerous. There was a tourist in Camden who was so shocked when drivers there stopped to let her cross, she had a massive coronary right there on Elm Street and died before the EMTs got her to the hospital.

Traffic circles

Here and there in Maine you will still find a few quaint "traffic circles." Ain't they cunnin'? The purpose of traffic circles is to keep traffic flowing at your busier intersections.

If you've never seen an authentic traffic circle you should seek one out and drive around it a few times (you really won't have a choice, you'll *have* to go around it a few times) just to say you did it and survived, assuming you do. These curious circles are sometimes called aortic aneurisms in Maine's arteries of traffic.

Other issues of importance

Cell phones:	You know that commercial where the geeky-looking guy is always asking, "Can you hear me now?" Well, the answer in Maine is, "No."
Inspection sticker:	Once an extra akin to heated seats, this sticker, proving that your vehicle is road-worthy, is now a necessity. In some parts of Maine, however, it is still possible to get a sticker on a rusted old Camaro for a six-pack.
Use of turn signals:	Mainers use them. Massachusetts drivers have apparently never heard of them and typically just use their middle finger.
Minimum driving age:	Automobiles, 16 years; more dangerous and difficult to drive vehicles, 5 years.
Right on red:	Yes, but please stop first.
Turn signals:	Please use them. Unlike Massachusetts, we have not banned them.

Service stations

Service? Not friggin' likely. Years ago we had service stations all over Maine. When you stopped for gas you got service. The folks who worked at these stations filled your tank, checked your belts, hoses, and fluids, took out a gauge to check your tire pressure and, after all that, they cleaned your windshield, smiling the whole time.

These days most gasoline in Maine is sold at so-called convenience stores—places where you pump your own fuel and clean your own windshield and nobody gives a damn about your belts, hoses, or fluids. Then, you go inside and stand in line while a dozen people in front of you buy Megabucks tickets and Marlboros. If nothing else, using the name "convenience" shows that the owners have a great sense of humor.

Traveling on a budget

Go to New Hampshire. Seriously. Or better yet, Vermont. They hate money in the People's Republic of Vermont.

In Maine, budget travel is absolutely impossible during the high seasons, i.e., seasons when anyone of sound mind and body would actually want to travel in Maine. In the olden days (let's say the 1980s and earlier) you sometimes could find a bargain at a local hotel if you looked hard enough. Today, all those hotels have either been condemned or bought, razed and replaced by giant, expensive resorts. Making matters worse is the creation of the "shoulder season." Now even fall and late spring are also out for budget travel along the coast. Inland, you might find a deal during mud season.

If you feel you must get away to Maine and don't want to spend a lot of money, you can look at places in, say, Bar Harbor or Rockport in mid-February. That $300-plus-per-night hotel will, if it is even open, charge a dite less. For probably something like $75, you could get a prime view of the barren, frozen bay, if visible at all through the artic sea smoke. Room service won't be available and most, if not all, of the top restaurants will likely be closed, but you can make a trip to the local country store for a six-pack and some premade Italian sandwiches.

So, if all you are looking for on your Maine getaway is to sit in a relatively inexpensive room with the shades pulled, eat a cold supper and watch cable television, well, I guess we do have a deal for you after all.

Currency

In parts of Maine, actual currency is used only when necessary. The preference is to barter, swap, dicker, and trade almost anything we have for something someone else might have—so make us an offer, and we'll talk.

My father was a dentist here in Maine, and as a kid I remember him trading bridge work for boats, or fillings for finish carpentry. Guests at both my sisters' weddings dined on lobster that my father traded for dental work.

If currency is used, the preference is cash, not checks or anything traceable. It helps out during tax season.

Weather

The year 1816 is known as the "The Year without Summah" in Maine. Now, an extra-sharp person might ask: "What in blue blazes is so odd about that?" And they would not be half wrong. But even

If you spend much time in small-town Maine, you'll notice that a native never uses the front door. It's quite possible that the front door is sealed year-round with plastic. It may not even have a doorstep. The surest way to let a Mainer know you are from away or with the Jehovah's Witnesses is to walk up and knock on the front door.

by Maine standards, 1816 was a bad one. That year measurable amounts of snow fell in every summer month, causing widespread crop failure, loss of livestock, a noticeable increase in tourist complaints and off-the-chart whining by tourist-related businesses. The local chamber of commerce in each town and the state's tourist bigwigs dismissed the snow in July as an illusion and blamed the media.

Anyway, I mention this as part of full disclosure so that when you plunk down your $350 a night for a beachfront room in Ogunquit in July and head out to catch some rays in your Speedo, you won't be completely shocked if it is snowing.

On the other hand, the skiing crowd, not to be confused with the skidder crowd, is always praying for a repeat of 1816, and that we'll get twelve straight months of snow to pump up their business.

The rest of us, however, like a break from snow. And fortunately for us, it's rare when we don't get at least thirty snow-free days in a row during a twelve-month period.

Weather in brief

January   Cold, snow, freezing rain, sleet.
Average temperature: Really cold
February   Same as January, only a tad colder and more unpleasant.
Average temperature: Wicked cold

March   Cold, but a dite less snow than February, which is
            offset by more sleet and freezing rain.
            Average temperature: Really wicked cold
April   Cold and damp with the added bonus of a bitter
            wind.
            Average temperature: Why is it still so damned
            cold?
May   Should be decent, but ain't. Often downright terrible.
            Average temperature: I can't believe it's still so
            damned cold.
June   Runs the gamut from cold and damp to nearly
            decent.
            Average temperature: Can you believe it's June and
            it's still this damned cold?
July   Hot and muggy in the morning, then foggy, cold
            and damp by sundown.
            Average temperature: Well, at least it's better than
            June, but this is still the worst July I can ever
            remember. It is so bad that there's no tourists and
            my sales are down at least 746 percent. I really
            don't know how I can stay in business any longer. I
            can barely pay my light bill.
August 11   Gorgeous! The reason we live in Maine.
            Average temperature: Pass the sunblock!
September   See August 11. Almost that good.
            Average temperature: You know, I felt quite a nip
            in the air this morning.
October   Still nice, but fading rapidly.
            Average temperature: I know it's Halloween, but
            you're just gonna have to wear your parka over your
            costume. What do you think this is, August 11?

November   Good weather for hunting, but little else. Descent
              to hellish weather begins in earnest.
              Average temperature: I just saw skim ice on the
              pond.
December   Snow is back in force and brings with it sleet,
              freezing rain, wind, and cold.
              Average temperature: Well, look on the bright
              side—only nine more months until August 11.

Maine weather—getting better all the time

Despite rumors to the contrary, we do have four main seasons in Maine. Of course, my friend Harold disagrees. He says we only have two: Winter and Three Months of Rough Sledding. Those three months, give or take, are also known as Tourist Season. But pay no attention to Wilbur. Maine's four seasons are Winter, Mud Season, Bug Season, and the fourth season, which has no official name, but is called alternately Leaf Season, Tourist-Go-Home Season, or Early Winter. We, of course, can't really count summer because it is typically confined to a single day in August. Although we are kind of hoping with all this talk of global warming that, someday, we may be able to stretch that out to two days, or maybe even a long weekend.

I'm sure you've heard a lot about our brutal winters, and you can rest assured that most of what you've heard is true. But apparently, the weather in Maine today is actually milder in all respects compared to the olden days.

When I was younger, my grandfather used to tell me about the tough winters of his day. I didn't know what cold was, he told me. And it wasn't just the winters. Summers today, he said, are much milder compared to the olden days when extreme heat was the norm.

Take the summer of 1889, August 13, I believe it was.

"It got so hot the ocean level dropped and folks could walk back and forth between the mainland and the islands—including Vinalhaven. For a while everyone thought it was some convenient and enjoyed not having to pay to ride the ferry," Gramps said.

"The ferryboats just leaned idle against their docks, and the sun beat down on them so bad they practically busted apart. Teamsters had more business than ever hauling things out to all the islands by wagon. All the ferry operators just about went bankrupt.

"For a while lobstermen could use wagons to get lobsters. They'd walk along beside their wagon and search for lobsters under the seaweed, and when they'd find them they'd pitch them in their wagon. But eventually it got so dry all the seaweed dried up, and the lobsters went offshore. Now, that was a dry summer, I tell you.

"Another summer," he said, "it was so hot one day that the corn growing in my cornfield began to pop right off the ears and sail into the air. The hot air carried the popped corn out over the cow pasture where it began to fall like snow. It's well

known that cows are not the brightest creatures on God's green earth, and as that popcorn began to fall into their pasture those numb cows thought it was real snow falling.

"Well, first they all began to shiver," he said, "thinking, as only cows can think, that if it's snowing it must be cold out. Before long every one of those cows froze to death right where they stood."

Accommodations

While driving through some of the more popular and therefore some of the most congested, traffic-clogged and overpriced parts of Maine (Route 1 from Wells to Biddeford; Route 1 from Northport to Bucksport; and anything on Route 3 east of Ellsworth), you'll get an idea of how fierce the competition is among motel and hotel owners that compete for your tourist dollars. That ferocious competition inspires many of these business owners to put up billboard-size marquees trumpeting their many attractions. Be prepared to drive past mile after mile of informational signs that brag about amenities like: POOL! CABLE TV! FREE LOCAL CALLS! COFFEEMAKERS IN ROOM!

As with anything else when competition is intense, some people will get carried away. If you are driving way Down East or in the western mountain region, you might see signs like: SHEETS & BLANKETS ON ALL BEDS! FREE SOAP & TOWELS! DOORS WITH LOCKS AND KEYS! FREE HOT & COLD WATER IN EVERY ROOM! TOILETS, SHOWERS & SINKS, OH MY!

It is in your best interest to carefully study and compare the lodgings offerings in Maine. In general, these are the types of accommodations you will find.

Bed & Breakfasts

If you like spending vacation time with total strangers and paying for the experience, you're a prime candidate for one of Maine's, quaint, cozy and costly B&Bs. You can't throw a stone without hitting one so you shouldn't have trouble finding one.

Our B&Bs are perfect for people who like their breakfast early in the morning, "garnished" (meaning cluttered) with strange-sounding herbs that you can't even pronounce, and for those who like to spend lots of money on lodging, but still enjoy sharing the dining area, sitting area, and sometimes bathrooms, with complete, and oftentimes annoying, strangers.

Cabins

I tell you, there's no better place to stay in Maine in summer than in a classic, no-frills cottage on the water—whether an ocean or a lake. Maine still has such cabins, and although they're not as plentiful as they once were, it's worth the effort to find one. Most come with small kitchens, or kitchenettes, comfortable living rooms and a couple of bedrooms. Some have screened-in porches, fireplaces, and a wood box filled with dry hardwood. Others have cobwebs, holes in the screens, families of ants in the cupboards, and outhouses. A little homework is in order.

Grand Hotels

Maine's oceanfront and lakes once had some of the grandest old hotels in the country. Some managed to survive and some were rebuilt after mysterious fires. People who have the time and money usually stay in one of these fine old places. If you can swing it, you should too. The drawbacks? Many of them are haunted. Really!

Inns

It's easy to confuse B&Bs with inns because so many B&Bs try their best to look like inns, and many Maine inns have been caught impersonating B&Bs. They cost about the same and offer almost identical services. The biggest difference, I guess, is in their names. Inns are also haunted.

Motel (non-chain)

What can I say? What can anybody say? We have lots of motels up one side of Maine and down the other, and we all have our favorite motel stories. Just don't expect a place called "Grand View Motel" to have anything approaching a grand view, unless it's of the parking lot. Randomly choosing a non-chain motel without any prior knowledge is a lot like Russian roulette; you may survive, you may even have a exhilarating time, but you might also—well, you know. Still, this is typically the most affordable option, *and* it may include—for free—entertainment such as the cops making a drug arrest or busting up a prostitution ring.

 Many hotels in Maine offer two types of rooms: Ocean View and Garden View. Ocean View in July and August will typically cost you about $1 million per night, not including taxes and gratuities. Garden View rooms are much cheaper. But be warned: When they say Garden View, don't think lovely flowers and tasteful benches; think pavement and garbage cans filled with rotting lobsters shells.

Motel/Hotel (chain)

Like a McDonalds in Moscow, these chain lodgings allow you to experience Maine without really experiencing Maine at all. Everything from the phrases used by the clerk during the check-in procedure to the brand of soap in the bathroom is exactly the same here in Maine as it would be in Montana. If there's one of the same chains in your hometown, you should just book yourself a room there and save yourself the gas money.

Resort & Spa

Those who want to spend some serious money just for a place to lay their weary heads will want to stay at a place with the words "resort" and "spa" in the name. What's a Resort & Spa? As near as I can figure, it's a hotel—that charges triple—where you can get your eyebrows waxed.

A newspaper in Maine once ran a personal ad that read: "Single woman with new boat and trailer seeks good man for companionship and possible relationship. All replies answered."

An intrigued man from Cherryfield wrote back: "I'm a single man and would be interested in relationship. Please send picture of boat."

Sporting camps

If you prefer the Maine highlands to the Maine Mall, you might want to check out one of the state's many sporting camps. After the logging crews got through with northern Maine and the trees began to grow again, sporting camps began to grow along with them. Some camps cater to wealthy sportsmen and provide things like personal guides who do everything from baiting your hook to filleting your catch and cooking it for your supper. If you want, they'll even catch the fish for you, allowing you to do what you do best—sit in your cabin at the sporting camp and drink.

Media

Daily newspapers

Maine has several daily newspapers, including those located in Bangor, Brunswick, Lewiston, and Portland. There may also be one somewhere in York County, but like I've said, most Mainers don't pay much attention to what's going on down there since it's just barely Maine. The daily paper in Portland is great if you like to read but don't actually want to find out anything about Maine. (You can get a more authentic local flavor of Maine in the *London Times* than in the Portland paper.)

But the fact is that people don't really pay as much attention to daily newspapers the way they used to (sort of like advertisers) except for the Jumble and Dilbert.

Weekly newspapers

If you actually want to get some local flavor and find out what is happening in the area where you are visiting, we suggest one of our many fine weekly newspapers. Many of us here in Maine like to have a week's worth of news all at once, which is why we have so many popular weeklies—from the *Ellsworth American* and *Machias Valley News Observer* to Newport's *The Rolling Thunder* and *The Notes* of Yarmouth. We like our weeklies a lot. Their staffs write news stories all week long and then they load them up and give you both barrels—blam, blam. And you really can find out a lot about the local culture, especially in the police beat.

Back home our local newspaper was *The Weekly Coastal Valley Harbor Record News Observer Review.* As you might have guessed, the paper was the result of the buying and selling and lumping together of several independent publications. Years ago, when even small Maine towns could support several newspapers, our little town had five: *The Weekly News, The Weekly Coastal Observer, The Valley News, The Weekly Review,* and *The Weekly Record.* After all the buying and selling and consolidating was done, we had one weekly newspaper with a name that took up most of the front page.

An Ellsworth man once observed: "We don't take the paper to see what's going on. We already know what's going on. We take the paper to find out who's getting caught at it."

There wasn't much "hard" news in our local paper, but there was all kinds of what they call soft news. Every week (hence the word "weekly" in the name) you'd get all the police and fire calls, engagements, weddings, births, obits, classifieds, and occasional reviews of one thing or another.

You can also find all you could ever want to know about fairs, festivals and other events in your weekly paper.

Free shoppers

Some people prefer newspapers that aren't all cluttered up with junk like news. They just want page after page of nothing but ads for everything from Cheerios to mufflers to lawn mowers to tanning salons—all with a heavy dose of community events tossed in.

Magazines

There was a time when Maine magazines used to have something to do with Maine. As peculiar as it sounds these days, they even wrote about Maine and the quirky individuals who actually lived here. But that was years ago. Now, they exist mostly to display multimillion-dollar homes for sale and to tell stories of the out-of-state millionaires who buy them or report breathlessly that a celebrity summering in Maine agreed to talk to them. Just once I'd like to see a cover story in one of these magazines like: "Maine's 10 Most Insufferable Landowners and the Unspeakable Things They're Doing to Our State."

Television

If you are visiting Maine, you should not be watching television.

The local angle

A critical element of any good Maine newspaper is finding the local angle to a national story. For example, when Congress passes a sweeping new law, it's often a big national story, but the editors of our weeklies will often ask, "How will this new law affect our readers here in Maine?" And then the editors will turn to a clueless staff writer and say something like, "Stop swilling that awful coffee of yours, Shlabotnik, and go out and get me a local-angle story on this new bill passed by those rascals in Congress," or words to that effect.

Sometimes the local angle will have to do with someone making national news who has some interesting local connection—"Oars for transatlantic rowing voyage made in Port

The proper way to break bad news while on vacation

One day, after many exhausting years of nonstop clamming, blueberry picking, and fishing, Wilbur Beal decided he was finally going to leave Washington County and take a vacation. There were all kinds of places in Maine he wanted to see, but had only read about—places like Island Falls and Jackman and Madawaska.

So Wilbur left his brother Liston to look after things, and he headed out for a two-week touring vacation.

The first day he got to Caribou, checked into a hotel, and called home to check on things. Liston answered the phone.

"How's everything back home, Liston?" Wilbur asked, getting right to the point of his call.

"Oh, things is okay, I guess," Liston said. After a short pause, he added, "Oh, by the way—your cat's dead."

The cat that Liston so bluntly reported dead was no ordinary cat. It happened to be a prized Maine Coon, and was probably the most valuable thing Wilbur owned.

Wilbur was some upset by Liston's report of the cat's demise. He said, "I just want you to know, Liston, that you've probably ruined my entire vacation, giving me such bad news on the first day out."

Liston said he was sorry, but he thought Wilbur should know about his cat.

"Of course I should know," said Wilbur. "But when someone's going to be on the road a week or two, and they call back the first night to see how things are, you don't hit 'um right between the eyes with the bad news all at once."

"Then how should I have told you?" Liston asked, all flustered.

"You should say something like: 'Your cat's up on the roof, and

she won't come down,'" said Wilbur. "That way I don't worry, see-
ings I know she's been on the roof before."

Wilbur continued, "The next night when I call, you say, 'We got
your cat off the roof, but we dropped her on her back and damaged
her vertebrae.' A little more serious, but I still think she'll pull
through. When I call next night, you say, 'Your cat's at the vet in serious condition.' The next night, you tell me she's in a coma. And on
the last night, you say my cat died quietly in her sleep. That's how
you break bad news to someone who's going to be on vacation for
two weeks. Understand?"

"Yes," Liston said, all apologetic and shameful. Next day, Wilbur
continued along on his vacation, driving up along the Canadian border to Fort Kent. After a good supper at the local country store,
Wilbur went back to his motel and called home to check on things.
Again, Liston answered.

"How are things back home?" Wilbur asked.

"Oh, things is okay, I guess," said Liston.

"That's good," said a relieved Wilbur. "And how's Mother?"

"Well, she's up on the roof," Liston said, "and she won't come
down."

Clyde" or, "Hot air for historic balloon trip came from *Portland
Press Herald* Editorial Offices."

Back in the late 1970s, when I was a reporter working for a
large northern Maine newspaper, there was what I consider a
classic local angle story that related to Pope John Paul II's visit
to Boston, some four hours south.

The Pope's historic visit—the first time a pope had ever visited New England—was a huge story, and the newspapers were
filled with all kinds of information about it. As expected, the
pope was greeted by large, enthusiastic crowds. But on the day

he said Mass on Boston Common the skies opened and it rained down cats and dogs. Unfortunate? Not for Maine.

The next day our paper had a big banner headline: POPE VISITS BOSTON, with several pictures of the pontiff and a long story about his historic visit. Below that lead story was a smaller story, featuring the local angle. It was headlined POPE'S RAINCOAT MADE IN BIDDEFORD.

Speaking the Language

Let's face it—most people who visit Maine talk a little funny. The accents we hear, oh my. Sometimes us Mainers can barely understand what you are trying to say. However, good communication can make everyone's stay in the Pine Tree State a tad more pleasant, so what follows is a brief primer to help you flatlanders communicate better as you move about our fair state.

Acre (a-kah)

A measure of land. If, after vacationing here for a while, you decide—like so many other tourists—to buy land in Maine, you should know right off that when we say "acre of land," we don't necessarily mean 44,240 square feet. A Maine acre is a mere suggestion, or figure of speech, if you will. In reality an acre can be almost any size. For that reason our Maine deeds will always contain the phrase "more or less" after any mention of something

Feuds over land in Maine are legendary. Down East, in Tremont, there was a man who wanted to divide his farm between his two sons. He sat at his kitchen table drawing a map and then got up and started to pace off the boundary from the edge of the kitchen table. He went right out the kitchen door to a large oak tree in the pasture and that line became the sons' boundary. Well, everything was hunky-dory until one day someone moved the kitchen table and a storm blew down the oak tree. The two sons have been feuding and haven't spoken since.

like "acreage." At the very least, it keeps the lawyers busy.

Alewife

A herring used for bait which can also be smoked. I've never smoked an alewife, but those who have say they're wicked hard to light.

Antiques

There was a time when antique furniture in Maine was known as "used stuff" and was sold in a "junk store." It wasn't until Summer Complaints started buying our old crap, filling their fancy cars with it, and hauling it back home to Massachusetts and New York that we realized how gullible people were, and therefore how valuable these old things were. "Junk" became "antiques" to be sold in antique shoppes. It is also a clever vertical integration. After we have a yard sale, we take what doesn't sell to an antique store—excuse me, shoppe—raise the price by 500 percent, and sell it there.

Ass-backwards

Completely wrong. "Would ya look at that. Billy's been away to the city too long; he tied up that boat ass-backwards."

Ass-over-teakettles

To fall or tumble. "No, Jess, no cribbage tonight; Mother's some sore. She went out to feed the hens, stepped on some ice and went down ass-over-teakettles."

Aya

When you hear someone mention "aya" they're talking about the stuff you have to breathe to stay alive. You'll appreciate Maine's clean air, unless you're breathing downwind from a local bait shed, paper mill or clamflats.

Ayuh

This is considered *the* word. When you hear "Aloha" you think of Hawaii; when you hear "Shalom" you think of Israel; when you hear a crude, unintelligible expletive you think New York; but when you hear someone say "Ayuh," it can only mean there's a Down Easter in the vicinity.

Tip: Although tourists too numerous to count have attempted to properly say *ayuh*, none has ever come close. If you should suddenly have the urge to try, don't. It's a Maine Thing.

Beam

On the coast of Maine, beam could be a) something holding up a house, or b) the width of a vessel, or c) the size of a large woman's backside.

"She's a fine woman, Chester, but you've got to admit, she's got some beam to her."

"There's no denying it," said Chester. "But she's warmth in the winter and shade in the summer."

Blowin' a gale

A fierce wind. "Didja go out today, Lewis?" "Hell no, it's blowin' a gale."

Bondo

Many cars in Maine, particularly those in northern and eastern Maine, are made substantially, if not entirely, of Bondo. These cars are easy to spot because the body, the hood and one of the doors are all a different color.

Calais

Pronounced KAH-liss, and don't let anyone tell you different. A fella from Machias was taking a friend from away for a drive to Calais and the friend kept insisting on mispronouncing it kah-LAY. Annoyed by this, the Machias fella pulled into the first store they came to in Calais. He dragged his friend into the store and said to the clerk, "Will you tell my friend here where we are?" The startled clerk answered: "True Value Hardware."

Can't miss it

Phrase typically uttered by someone Down East after giving directions to a tourist. Loosely translated, it means: "Ain't no way in hell you are going to find it, chummy."

Chain saw

A chain saw is to rural Mainers what a hose is to a firefighter, or what grossly overpriced coffee is to someone from Cambridge—a necessity. In rural Maine, the chain saw is used to clear land, cut up firewood, get a raccoon out of a tree, build a house, do finish carpentry, and carve the ice sculpture for a local wedding. And, no Maine fair or festival would be allowed to operate without at least one chain-saw artist.

Chips

Be careful to pay attention to how it's used in a sentence. That's because here in Maine we have our fish and chips, our wood chips and our cow chips—each important in their own way, but not to be confused.

Christer (christ-ah)

A big storm, big event, or grand idea.

Country

If a Mainer lives on a road where the trailers are three miles apart, that person will say he lives in the country. But that neighborhood will seem congested to someone who lives on a road where the trailers are ten miles apart. We knew folks who lived seventeen miles down a dirt road and no one else lived on the road, but when they went to their camp up north they always said they were "going to the country."

County, The

Aroostook. No other name is necessary. If you say to someone, "I am going up to The County" and they say, "Which one?" You know you're talking to an out-of-stater or someone from Portland.

Cunnin'

If someone calls your child cunnin', they don't mean the little rascal is wily, crafty, and sneaky; they mean your kid is wicked cute. It's a compliment, so enjoy it. If a Mainer looks into your baby carriage and says, "You can't deny that one," that has a whole different meaning, so move on.

Cupsuptic

If you're renting a cottage by a lake and your host uses the word "Cupsuptic" in a sentence, you might think they're talking about the plumbing—as in "I'm afraid I'm going to have to replace the entire cupsuptic system under the cabin." But Cupsuptic is a lake near Mooselookmeguntic, which is a word sometimes used to clear a piece of moose meat from your throat.

Daow (d-ow)

Emphatic "No," while at the same time trying to be "playful and engaging." In fact, it's about as emphatic and playful a negative as you're likely to hear along the coast. In Maine courts the word "daow" is officially recognized as a negative response to a question. However, if you start using this common Maine word in other jurisdictions, it may not always work unless you have this reference book with you to show the judge. "Didja pay a lot for the new pickup?" "Daow, I got a helluva deal."

Dear (dee-ah)

All-purpose term used as sort of a nickname for anyone regardless of age, sex, or profession.

Dicker (dick-ah)

To haggle. It's also considered a way of being sociable. If you visit a yard sale while you're here—and you'll have many to choose from—be prepared to dicker for most every item you want. When dickering, seller and buyer go through an ancient and pleasantly elaborate series of offers and counteroffers until a price is eventually arrived at. Often the more worthless the item, the more intricate and complicated the dickering.

"How much for those broken clothespins and bent hangers?"

"Fifty cents."

"I'll give you twenty."

"How 'bout twenty-five?"

"Sold."

Dite

A little. If a waitress asks: "Would you like some cream in your coffee?", you should say, "Just a dite, deah."

Dooryard

This is synonymous with front yard. No matter how large or small a Maine house might be, there are always those things that won't fit inside. Those important items—old washers and dryers, engine blocks, tires, trannys and other vital car parts, sound systems, various types of gas- and woodstoves, sofas, box springs and the like—can be neatly "stored" in a dooryard.

Down East

Few people these days can explain why a place that's up north should be called "Down East." Fewer still have any idea what Down East means and where Down East begins. I once asked someone who had just moved to Portland if he'd ever been Down East. He said, "I've been to Freeport."

Some say you've got to go at least as far as Rockland before you can talk about being Down East. In Rockland, they say you can't even get a whiff of Down East until you get to Belfast. In Belfast, they say it begins in Ellsworth, and in Ellsworth they say you want to go to Milbridge if you want to be Down East. Milbridge residents insist you go to Eastport. And in Eastport, they are just happy to see anyone.

Duct tape

Miracle product that can be used for everything from patching up a tent to open heart surgery.

Eavesdrop

If you find yourself in a colorful diner Down East and you decide to eavesdrop on the nearby tables, you might find—if you know the language—that the locals are talking about *you!*

Far (fah)

Opposite of near, but a distance that could be one mile to 500 miles. If you ask someone: "How far is it to Bangor?" they may say something like, "Not far." If you press them and say, "But how many miles is it?" They will say, "Not far."

Farm (fahm)

A piece of rocky ground surrounded by stone walls where the only thing a farmer can grow is tired, and eventually sell the place to a lawyer from Boston. An Aroostook County farmer once won $3 million in the Megabucks drawing, and when a reporter asked what he was going to do with all the money, he said, "I'll probably keep farming until it's all gone."

Finest kind

General term for good or excellent. "How's them fish heads?" "Finest kind."

Fish or cut bait

Do something!

Fog

A local weather phenomenon used to drive tourists into gift shops and malls.

Free range

Some say it has to do with hens that aren't penned up. It could also mean an electric stove you found down at the dump that just needs a little tinkering.

Friggin'

Expletive. "Ain't no friggin' way I'm going down to the boat today. That friggin' Clyde has gone and frigged up the engine so the friggin' boat won't even friggin' start. It's too friggin' cold anyway."

Gawmy

Clumsy, awkward.

Get your bait back

When fishing or lobstering, your goal is to get back a catch at least equal in value to the bait used to catch it. When someone uses a load of bait to catch a small mess of fish, it's said, "He barely got his bait back." Don't be surprised to hear the expression used to describe a smaller-than-average baby. "Did you see Hollis's new baby? I'd say he barely got his bait back on that one."

Gettin' by

Statement used to describe a person's income, whether they are poor or rolling in cash. A mill worker who says he is gettin' by probably means he is making enough money to pay the bills. When a lobster fisherman says he's gettin' by, it probably means he's made so much money he's about to pay cash for a $32,000 pickup truck so he can haul his 40-inch plasma TV home.

Grange

As you travel through Maine you'll see lots of old Grange Halls. The Grange movement came to Maine around 1873, and since then has had its ups and downs. Lately it's been mostly down. In some Maine Grange Halls in summer you'll find entertainment, bean suppers, auctions, flea markets, and such. In others you probably won't find much of anything.

Guess probably (guess prob'ly)

Emphatic "Yes!" sometimes tinged with sarcasm. "What's that smell? You been eatin' beans again?" "Guess prob'ly!"

Gunwales (gunn'lls)

The top plank of a vessel that used to have guns bolted to it. A Mainer says something like: "When she left the cove and headed for Rockland she was loaded right to the gunn'lls with sardines." Which means she barely had a plank showing above the waterline.

You might also hear a Mainer use the term in a non-nautical reference. "I was just down to the True Value and they were having such a great sale on paint that I filled my pickup right up to the gunn'lls with about fifty gallons of the stuff."

Gut

(1) *noun*: A place known as a gut is just barely suitable as a harbor or anchorage. The picturesque Knox County village of Port Clyde was known to early fishermen as "Herring Gut" until Summer Complaints started buying up cottages in the area. They didn't like writing to their friends in Boston, New York, and Philadelphia and putting "Herring Gut, Maine" as their return address. So they started a move to change the name to Port Clyde. But to locals it will always be known fondly as "Herring Gut." (2) *verb*: to clean and prepare a fish for cooking or drying.

Heirship property

If you're interested in buying real estate here in Maine, you should know the meaning of this term. "Heirship property" is what results when all the members of a far-flung family have some claim to a nice piece of property. In order to tidy up the deed, some lawyer has to draw up complicated legal papers and have every last one of those far-flung relatives sign off on whatever claim—if any—he or she has on the property in question. Depending on how many relatives there are and how much money you're willing to spend, you might be able to straighten the whole thing out in the amount of time you have left on this earth. Heirship property is the cause of some of the longest-running feuds in Maine. You'd be surprised how attached and ornery someone from Ohio can become over 1/132nd of an acre.

Hod (hawd)

A hod is used by clammers to tote clams. A clammer who can't find his might say, "Gawd, ain't that awd; I thought I'd left my hawd right heah."

Italian

A type of sandwich that is more Maine than Italian, but we like them.

Jeezely

A Maine word that can be used as an adjective or an adverb, but if you have to ask what it means, you have no jeezely business using it.

Jet ski

Warm-weather snowmobile. It is a machine that really annoys rich out-of-staters who prefer *not* to be reminded that there are locals within 50 miles of their lakefront summer cabin.

Jonesport (jones-pawt)

We don't know what to say about Jonesport. It just didn't seem right to be talking about Down East words and not include Jonesport.

Labor Day

As a kid I was always told that Labor Day was a Maine creation designed to get rid of tourists. The rule was, by Labor Day all summer visitors had to have their boats out of the water, their camps closed up tight, and the whole family on the 'pike headed someplace south—no excuses! The rule worked fine until a few years ago when—after some years of lax law enforcement—the tourist gurus in Augusta created the "Shoulder Season" so that tourists started staying a little longer each year. Shoulder Season is basically a polite term for "The weather sucks."

Lee

Out of the wind. "It's some friggin' cold." "Well, knuckle-head, go stand in the lee and you'll be warmer."

Lighthouse

One of the Holy Trinity of Maine tourist icons, along with Moose and Lobster. Once used to guide sailors but now used to attract tourists. Merchants in Maine know that the best way to attract a tourist is with a representation of a moose, a lobster, or a lighthouse. If you are a shopkeeper having trouble trying to sell a brown suede jacket with pink fringes, polka-dot collar, and a purple rhinestone-studded pocket, just iron on a picture of a lighthouse and watch it fly!

Lobster (Lob-stah)

The food and *the* icon. Known in scientific circles as *Homerus americanus*—which we think is Latin for humorous American. One of the Holy Trinity of Maine Icons. See also Moose and Lighthouse.

Lottery (law-tree)

A voluntary tax on mostly poor people who tend to be unlucky. Usually bought in set with beer and cigarettes.

Mess

(1) Trouble. "He sure has gotten himself in a mess." (2) A lot. "I think I will go pick a mess o' greens."

Moose

The third part of the Holy Trinity of Maine Tourism icons. See also Lobster and Lighthouse.

Mount Desert Island

It's Mount Dih-ZERT (the sweet treat served after supper), not Mount DEH-zert (an arid land with little vegetation).

Muckle

Grab ahold and hang on for all she's worth.

Numb as a haddock

Especially stupid. "That Billy Carpenter is numb as a haddock, I tell you. There are some people who don't know nawthin', but that friggin' Billy don't even suspect nawthin'."

Old Orchard Beach

If you prefer greasy fried dough and vulgar T-shirt emporiums to bold rocky cliffs and picturesque fishing villages, you'll want to head for Old Orchard as soon as you can.

Pine tree

What the longhorn is to Texas, the pine tree is to Maine. In olden days, the pine tree was more recognizable as a state icon than the Moose, Lobster, and Lighthouse. But we cut them all down.

Pirate

The vendors on the interstate are the latest practitioners of this ancient trade, but Maine has been home to such famous pirates as Samuel Bellamy and Captain Kidd.

Scrid

A teeny bit. Even smaller than a dite.

Self-employed

Code for "I don't pay any taxes." Here in Maine it could mean that the person digs clams or bloodworms.

Shedder

A soft-shelled lobster.

Snow

Because we're so far north, you're right in assuming we have many words for snow; but since this book is meant for family reading, we can't list the most common.

Trailer

Part of the answer to the question: What do a Maine divorce and a Florida hurricane have in common? Either way, some poor fella's going to lose his trailer.

Transplant

Someone from away who has moved to Maine. If you see someone driving a Peugeot with a DON'T STEAM LOBSTERS bumper sticker on the back, it's almost certain the driver is a transplant. Tends to stick out like a sore thumb.

Unorganized township

Maine's always had more land than people to fill it, so the patches of land that are left over are called "unorganized townships." Not to be confused with our disorganized townships.

Warp (whop)

Nothing to do with my sense of humor. "Warp" is what they call the line on a lobster trap.

Wicked (wik-id)

Adjective. "How's the ice cream?" "Wicked good!"

Maine Translations

Maine	Flatlander
punt	dinghy or rowboat
lobster car	lobster pound
bait	sushi
Mother	wife
dinner	lunch
Ah	R
foolish	PETA
barrens	blueberry fields
whore's egg	sea urchin
frappe	milkshake (with ice cream)
jimmies	sprinkles
L.L. Bean	Maine
North Massachusetts	York County

Maine Cuisine

As you might expect, Maine has a bushel-full of unique foods—some extraordinary and some I would not touch with a 10-foot pole. To steal a line from someone else, it seems parts of Maine cuisine were based on a dare, and others on a coronary.

Lobster

The Maine food. No others need apply. As we said earlier, the popularity of lobsters is a testament to nineteenth-century marketing that took what was essentially a trash item and turned it into a high-priced delicacy. Brilliant. Can be served in the shell, in lobster rolls, in stews, stuffed, or any of a hundred different ways. The most authentic way, though, is steamed in a pot and served with melted butter, cole slaw, and a roll.

How about some PETA in melted butter?

It has been a long-simmering debate, and people on both sides can get pretty steamed up by it, you might say.

The question? Do lobsters feel pain when they are thrown live into a pot and steamed?

Millions of lobster lovers—like me—say, "Who cares? Pass the butter, please."

Busybodies who don't want you to enjoy a nice lobster dinner say, "Yes! End the suffering! Let lobsters live!"

Every summer at the Maine Lobster Festival, the good people of Rockland gather at the public landing to have a wonderful time steaming some fifty thousand pounds of live lobsters for tens of thousands of hungry people.

A few years back, a Virginia-based group called People for the Ethical Treatment of Animals (PETA) arrived in Rockland to protest the cooking and eating of lobsters, and, as such groups are wont to do, to make everyone feel guilty.

PETA members walked around downtown demonstrating and passing out recipes for more correct foods—yummy items like Seaweed Supreme and Dulce Delight. Mmm-mmm! Some PETA people even marched up and down Main Street in bright red lobster costumes handing out informational brochures. Happy, hungry festivalgoers standing in line for lobster dinners, thinking the costumed demonstrators were from Maine's Lobster Promotion Council, waved and smiled at them. After all, everyone knows that red is the color of a cooked lobster. The costumed PETA people were darned lucky, come to think of it, that none of those hungry people in line tried to crack off one of their claws.

At long last, the findings of a fancy scientific study funded by the Norwegian government should put an end to the argument. The study concluded that "No brain, no pain" is true. Lobsters have brains the size of a grain of sand (or was that PETA they were talking about?), and therefore don't have the necessary equipment to feel pain. A lobster might feel uncomfortable, like people feel on a hot, crowded subway car, but it feels no pain.

Fish fry

It's a down payment on a heart attack, but you still shouldn't leave Maine without going to an authentic Down East fish fry.

If you like healthy, simply broiled fresh fish—cod, haddock, flounder, sole, whiting—look elsewhere; but if you are looking for fish cooked in dripping-fresh 30-weight oil, the kind of oil that really lubricates your moving parts, you sure want to try and get to a Maine fish fry. Look in any newspaper for dates and times and put the ambulance on speed dial.

Fried dough

If you want the fish-fry experience without the smell and taste; if you want pure, artery-clogging fat with no distractions, or even accidental health benefits—and you want it fast—then you need fried dough. Basically, a big glob of carbs dripping in 40-weight oil. And in Maine, it should be coated white with powdered sugar.

Red hot dogs

Maine is probably the only place in North America where you can legally manufacture, possess, and foolishly consume hot dogs that are blazingly and brazenly and unapologetically bright red. They look a little like road flares and some people (Transplants mostly) might argue they taste just a tad worse. You know they are authentic if after you boil them in a small pot, the water is fire-engine red.

The way we heard the story, a bunch of guys were sitting around the break room at a hot dog factory in Brewer when they began wondering aloud what they could do to make their hot dogs a tad more deadly.

Tip: If you are looking for the best hot dogs, some of my favorite places are: Bolly's in Augusta, Danny's in Brunswick, Wasses in Rockland, and Lonnie's in Gray.

After shooting down a number of ideas involving needles and balloons, one guy spoke up and said, "How about we add a fifty-gallon drum of red dye number ten to each batch?" "Genius!" came the reply.

There are several ways to prepare these special treats, but we think the two most authentic are: steamed (along with white-bread rolls) in a special hot dog steaming contraption in the parking lot of some place such as the local IGA, and served with a healthy dose of onions, relish, mustard, and ketchup; or stuck on the end of a whittled stick and cooked over a campfire or bonfire until charred. The benefit of the latter is that if cooked correctly, your hot dog can be burnt on the outside and stone-cold on the inside.

The Maine Italian

Some say Maine's Italian sandwich was invented during World War I at a take-out restaurant near a shipyard on Portland's waterfront. Others say it was first assembled in the

1950s in the shadow of Westbrook's paper mill. No matter who says what, the idea of putting the delicious combination of ham, cheese, tomato, green peppers, onions, black olives and olive oil smack dab in the middle of a nice, long, soft roll has been around for quite a few years, and has been popular among the best of us for just as many.

On the menu in some of your fancier Maine restaurants, you will often see an item called Soup du Jour. Now, I have nothing against most French food, but the problem I have with this is that you never know what it is going to be from one day to the next.

Why not try an authentic Maine Italian sandwich and let us know what you think? They're pretty cheap, too, for you budget-conscious tourists.

Moxie

Moxie was invented in Maine—Lisbon Falls, to be exact. Based on recent actions of the Maine Legislature, Moxie is now the official drink of Maine. (I think they may have been worried about the images of the previous unofficial drinks: coffee brandy and milk, and hard cider.) We should be clear on one thing before we continue: Moxie tastes awful. At best it is an acquired taste, and usually acquired only after you have destroyed your taste buds with years of fried food.

Amazingly, Moxie was originally billed as an elixir—a health tonic—and I guess if there's one thing Maine people need from time to time, it's a powerful health tonic.

Pickled eggs

For those who are not familiar with the delicacy, pickled eggs are shelled, hard-boiled eggs floating in a murky brine, an awful-looking liquid that's a half-step from toxic waste these days.

Large jars of pickled eggs once sat on the counters of almost every little variety store in Maine. I remember staring at them and wondering how reckless or drunk you'd have to be to reach in and grab one. Gauging the haziness of the liquid, I'd also try and guess how long those particular eggs had been in the jar, and I'd try to picture what the person would look like who would snatch the last egg. I don't want to get graphic here, but I can tell you that the specimens in the jars in my high school science lab looked a lot more appetizing than any jar of pickled eggs I ever saw.

About the only good thing you can say about a jar of pickled eggs is that the vinegar brine is so strong, it would probably kill most of the bacteria on the hand of the customer who preceded you.

Tripe

I think tripe is less popular than it used to be, thank goodness. Tripe is the muscular lining of beef stomach and could be described as a gelatinous and blond membrane that is tough to digest. Ideally it's cooked some twelve hours. Mmmm.

Sardines

Small ocean fish packed, bones and all, into a tin with a variety of sauces so it become mushy. Best to eat straight from the tin, no knife or fork, so the juice and sauce gets on your fingers and shirt.

Casseroles

Several types of food mixed together in a dish and baked. A staple of rural Maine. For the best public casseroles, head off to the local Baptist or Congregational Church.

Pickled pigs' feet

You want to talk about nasty, mister man. We believe these are also associated with the South, but you can find them here too, sometimes right on the counter next to the pickled eggs. They are eaten as a snack right out of the jar that contains a brine that gives pickled-egg brine a run for its money. Pickled pigs' feet are salted and smoked, and then placed in jars and covered with a solution of hot brine containing vineger. The brine tends to congeal a bit just to ratchet up the nasty-factor.

Fish heads

Every time I went to see my old Aunt Ella at the nursing home, she would say, "Next time, why don't you bring me a mess o' fried fish heads." Because I would have been sick? A staple of old-time coastal Maine, these are just what the name implies. Fish heads, eyeballs and all, fried up in a pan.

Kipper snacks

Snack food usually made of herring (bones and all). My problem with eating herring stems from the fact that herring is also used for lobster bait. Well, that, and it's gross.

Whoopie pies

Perhaps the most unhealthy, thus popular, Maine pastry available. We have never made these, but the recipe calls for a slab of Crisco mixed with sugar smushed between two round pieces of chocolate cake. Twinkies are for weenies.

Salt pork

This slab of animal fat was a staple of old-time Maine. It could be added to any dish to "grease it up," i.e., make it even more unhealthy. Salt pork might be diced, fried in a skillet, and added to meat dishes, or sliced into strips and added to greens, just to mention two uses. It's very popular in baked beans.

Butter

Real Mainers believe that butter (*not* a butter substitute) should never be used in any measure of less than a brick. A piece of toast? A brick of butter. A biscuit? A brick of butter. A bowl of macaroni? A brick of butter.

Ketchup

The Maine food equivalent of duct tape. Can be used to improve virtually any dish and should be used in large quantities. In lieu of sauce, my Uncle Abner used to pour half a bottle into a bowl of elbow macaroni. Stir and enjoy.

Fried clams

Now, if you are a real Mainer, you don't want anything wimpy—you want clams in crumbs, not batter, and with bellies intact. Clam strips are for nancy-boys. The only garnishment necessary (required, actually) is tartar sauce. Clam shacks are everywhere in Maine, and you can rest assured that health inspectors regulary check the deep-fat fryers to ensure the highest quality of fat available.

Steamed clams

Steamed clams are also a quintessential Maine food, Red Tide be damned. Should be steamed, rinsed in hot clam broth, then dipped in butter or vinegar and eaten with often-gritty and always-mushy bellies intact.

Corn chowder

A curious Maine winter dish. No meat. No fish. Just milk broth, potato, onion, and corn, mostly. Can be found only at restaurants that specialize in "home-cooked" fare.

Dried codfish

Dried cod was once a staple of Maine. The catching, drying and shipping of cod largely built parts of the Maine coast. Today it is a delicacy, in many eyes, anyway. It can be purchased at some local stores, but the authentic way to eat dried fish is to catch a cod, clean it, split it, and either hang it by the tail or lay it inside a lobster trap to dry in the sun. When it is ready, just cut out the worms with a jackknife, strip the dried meat off the skin, and enjoy. Classic.

Dulce

Essentially, purple seaweed. Islanders and coastal folks collect it along the beach or floating in the water, hang it up on clotheslines or in the boat to dry, then eat it as a snack.

American chop suey

This concoction of macaroni (elbows), tomato sauce, and ground beef has, obviously, nothing to do with chop suey of the Chinese persuasion. It should really be called Maine chop suey if it's called chop suey at all, because I've yet to see it on the menu anywhere else in America. You'll find American chop suey at bean suppers, at diners, and in school cafeterias. It's wildly popular at all three venues.

Local establishments

There are a lot, and I mean a lot, of fantastic restaurants in Maine. But if you want a true local flavor, some of my favorites (for real!) are: Dysart's Truck Stop in Hermon, A-1 Diner in Gardiner, Moody's Diner in Waldoboro, Lunt's Dockside Deli in Frenchboro, Miss Wiscasset Diner in Wiscasset, Becky's in Portland, Cole Farms in Gray, Jasper's in Ellsworth, Helen's in Machias, and Red Barn in Milbridge.

Just like home

Thelma Ames, a solid Columbia Falls woman, used to write food reviews for the local paper. She did a bang-up job. If she liked the food, it was good. If she didn't, you wouldn't. Simple as that.

In one review of a supper at the Odd Fellow's Hall, Thelma captured the experience beautifully when she wrote, "Although I've never done time in our county jail, I suspect that a plate of this sublime American Chop Suey could easily transport a felon back to a jail's dining hall, if only for a moment."

Boy, could that woman write.

I thought about our hometown paper and Thelma's reviews the other day after reading about all the publicity Maine's been getting lately in some of those glossy national magazines, with names like *Bon Appétit*, *Wine Spectator*, and *Today's Clammer*. They've written all kinds of things about Portland's Old Port that to me are just plain silly.

A *Bon Appétit* writer said of a Portland restaurant, "Spending time there is like being transported to New York's East Village."

Now, correct me if I'm wrong, but I've always assumed that magazines like your *Bon Appétit* and the rest are read mostly by people stuck in places like New York's East Village. So why would a sophisticated New Yorker want to drive eight or nine hours north to Portland on congested roads in order to eat at a place that's just like the restaurants right there in New York?

You'd think that people spending all that time and money to get up here to Maine would want to experience something you couldn't get back in the big city. Like a nice plate of the American Chop Suey Thelma wrote about.

If I were up here from New York, I can tell you what I'd do. I'd grab the first bright red steamed Maine hot dog I could find; I'd stop for a bite at Dysart's Truck Stop in Hermon or the Miss Wiscasset Diner; or I'd really push the gastronomic envelope and chow down at a bean supper somewhere way Down East.

Bon appétit, indeed.

Activities and Entertainment

It doesn't take much to entertain us in Maine. As I've already mentioned, you tourists do a pretty good job of amusing us without even really trying. Yes, we've got bars and dance halls and cinemas and theaters, but hey, you're in Maine. You can do that at home; but I bet you can't go play Cow Chip Bingo or watch lobster boat races.

You can't go a summer day in Maine without a fair or a festival scheduled. The Fourth of July, with its attendant parades and fireworks, is of course a popular date, but then there's Rockland's Lobster Festival, Yarmouth's Clam Festival, Portland's Old Port Festival, and the Lisbon Falls Moxie Festival. And don't forget about the rollicking Blackfly Festival, the Rumford Vacant Building Festival, The Potato Blossom Festival, the Bloodworm Festival, the Surimi Festival, the

PAPETA (People Against PETA) Festival, the Meddybemps
Festival and the list goes on. Likewise, our fairs are just too
numerous for me to provide between these covers a comprehen-
sive list. Counties have fairs, churches have fairs, crafters have
fairs, worm diggers have fairs. You get the picture.

Fourth of July parades

There's a town in Maine that boasts of having the largest
Fourth of July parade per capita of any town or city in Maine.
Trouble is, the town is so small and the parade is so large that
by the time the organizers get the Grand Marshal and his
entourage in place, then line up the Gold Star Mothers, the
folks in town who own antique cars, the American Legion and
its auxiliary, the VFW and its auxiliary, the 4-H and its advi-
sors, the Masons, the Knights of Columbus, the Boy Scouts, the
volunteer firemen and their auxiliary, the high school band, the
middle school band, the elementary school band, the Little
League teams, Babe Ruth teams, Farm Team, T-Ball tots,
Young Farmers of America, and a lot of other, incidental
marchers—well, there's no one left in town to watch the parade.

When that huge parade goes sailing down Main Street, there
won't be one soul on the sidewalk watching it.

It got so bad that they had to ask Fred Peasely from the
public-access station in a town downriver to come tape the
parade and put it on cable so the townspeople could finally get
a look at it.

Cow Chip Bingo

Cow Chip Bingo is a classic in parts of Maine and other agricultural areas. Basically, it works like this: You take a large

field, line it off to create dozens of squares, and assign numbers to those square boxes. People take turns buying/betting on one of the numbers. Once the squares are sold out, a cow is let loose in the field. When the cow does her business, whichever square it lands in is the winning number. These are special events, so watch the papers carefully.

Wife Carrying Competition

In Maine, you may notice small wiry men weighing no more than 135 to 140 pounds paired up with women who weigh close to 300. Why is that, you may ask.

It may not be politically correct to say this, but young men Down East are advised to marry large women—they'll provide shade in summer, warmth in winter.

With that in mind, if you're a male who likes beer and money (Duh) and you're planning to be here in Maine on Columbus Day weekend, you might want to check out the annual Wife Carrying Championship in Newry. This is the heart of Maine's ski country, but the contest is much more popular with the skidder crowd than the ski crowd.

Males must run an obstacle course that includes jumping over hurdles and sloshing through waist-high water while carrying their wife, girlfriend, or other adult female on their back. The winner receives the woman's weight in beer and five times her weight in cash.

So if Mother dresses out at the preferred weight of 250 to 300 pounds, you could win enough beer for the first quarter of your average Patriots game, and a pile of cash for good measure.

A festival's a good bet

Like all good Maine Yankees, Sherm Ames knew how to squeeze a dollar, and was loathe to part with a penny if there was any good way to avoid it.

One year, he and his wife, Thelma, were at one of the seafood festivals on the coast watching the tourists and seeing the sights, when they came upon a fella giving open-style airplane rides for $20 each. The man promised a magnificent sky-high view of the rocky coastline and a sprinkling of nearby islands.

Neither Sherm nor Thelma had ever had a sky-high view of the coast before, so they were both mighty curious. But, neither did they have anything like $40 between them, since they had mostly come just to see the sights, as I said, and so far in Maine, that doesn't require much cash.

Now the pilot wasn't doing much business on this day, so he thought he'd have a little sport with Sherm and Thelma. He said, "Listen, mister, I'll take you and your wife for a ride in my plane. And if you can sit through the entire ride without saying a word, the ride will be free."

Sherm didn't know anything about plane rides, but he knew that was no bet to make with a Down Easter. It took a lot to fluster Sherm and he'd gone months without uttering a word, relying on just a reverse nod when absolutely necessary. So, Sherm took the wager. Within minutes the pilot and Sherm and Thelma were flying high above the rocky shore. Once the pilot achieved top altitude, he began a steep, frightening nosedive. A second before potential impact with the crashing waves, the pilot pulled out of the dive and soared back into the sky.

Sherm sat there quiet as a church mouse. It would take more than near death to get him to open his mouth.

Before long the pilot was doing loop-de-loops, fancy leaf-falls and barrel rolls, and every other scary trick he could think of.

Sherm remained stone-silent.

Finally, the pilot realized he was just wasting fuel and he wasn't going to make Sherm talk, so he brought his plane in for a landing.

After they touched down, the pilot, one-part aggravated, one-part impressed, turned to Sherm and said, "Wasn't there a single time during that ride when you felt like saying anything at all?"

Sherm sat for a moment and said, "Well, truth be told, I did have to bite my tongue when Mother fell out, but otherwise, no."

The county fair

If you're here during county fair season, you're in luck. Fair time in late summer and early fall is my favorite time of year. Whether the weather is fair or foul, I wouldn't miss any of it.

Years ago my parents used to pack up our whole family and head for the county fair. Every year there was some special attraction that was more exotic than the year before. Some years it would be something like a bearded lady. These days I suppose they'd have to call her "follically gifted" or some such foolishness. Other years it would be something like the World's Fattest Person or the World's Greatest Ventriloquist. It was all mighty impressive stuff.

Occasionally the outlandish acts would cause some confusion. One year someone in town thought the World's Greatest Ventriloquist was in fact an expert on air ducts and ventilation and that sort of thing. Ned, a DIY-er before it was popular, was in the middle of renovating his kitchen and needed some advice. You can imagine he was some upset after buying a ticket and sitting through an entire show of this fella sitting there talking to a dummy.

Most of the time, though, folks went away pretty impressed and would talk about the fair for days afterwards.

One year the main attraction was a world champion bull that according to the advertisement in the newspaper had come all the way from Mexico. A fella in town who was a bit slow to understand said: "I don't know what's such a big deal about this bull being all the way from Mexico. I've been over to Rumford and Mexico lots of times."

"They're not talking about Mexico, Maine, Hollis," our town's local expert replied. "This isn't a Maine bull, Hollis; this champion bull is from some other Mexico down in the southwest somewhere," the expert explained.

Apparently, someone had put this magnificent bull in a fancy truck with all kinds of special bull attendants to take care of him, just like a pampered rock star, and they were touring around the whole country going to all the county fairs. When they arrived at a new location, the highly trained attendants would go right to work and set up a special tent for the bull, complete with a show ring and grandstands and fresh sawdust on the ground. And, I kid you not, the bull even had groupies who went from town to town and show to show. What can I say? Even back then some people just had too much free time on their hands.

Anyway, once my thirteen siblings and I heard about that champion bull, we sure wanted to see it. On the big day, the family—Father, Mother and us fourteen kids—piled into our old car and drove down to the fairgrounds. We started talking about which food booths we wanted to visit first.

To make sure you got a balanced diet at the fair, you needed to offset your huge sheets of fried dough, steamed red hot dogs, and large boxes of onion rings with a few large wads of sticky cotton candy. The more health-conscious types would want to add a vegetable, so they'd just add a pile of those greasy French fries to the mix. Since it was summertime, most of the frying at the fair was done, of course, in your lighter-weight 10w30 cooking oil.

This particular year, the year of the champion bull, there were so many people at the fair that we had to park more than a mile from the grounds. But we all knew it would be worth it.

When we came up to the ticket booth to buy our tickets, we noticed the sign on the bull's giant tent that read SEE THE CHAMPION BULL, 10 CENTS.

Now, 10 cents doesn't seem like a whole lot of money these days, but back in the 1950s it was, especially when you had to multiply it by the sixteen people in our family.

Father, a true Down Easter, was always looking for ways to save money.

So, while we stood to one side, Father went up to the man selling tickets and said, "You don't suppose my family and I could get in on a special group rate, do ya?"

The man looked at my father; then he turned and looked at my mother and then at us fourteen children stretched out behind the two of them.

Slowly, this fella reached into his own pocket, took out a dime, handed it to my father and said, "Never mind that, mister. You stand right there. I'm bringing that bull out to see *you*."

Outdoor Recreation

If you are coming to Maine, you should probably get outside at least once for a little activity and to enjoy nature. Here are a few suggestions/helpful hints.

Birding

Maine's most visible feathered friends—by far—are seagulls, which spend most of their time at our better dumps. Hey, everybody's got to eat. For those who like to have lots of different birds around to look at, we hear you. There are many more birds for your watching and hunting pleasure. Just keep your eyes open; you'll find them. (It may seem like a small matter, but make sure the bird you're hunting is in season. Game wardens are funny about those things, and I don't mean funny, ha-ha.)

 If peace and quiet is what you are looking for, there are many great places to find it in Down East Maine. Some may find the degree of peace and quiet to be a little too much, though. It has been said that one coastal town in Washington County is so dull, the tide went out one day and never came back.

Biking

In some parts of Maine, biking is an accident waiting to happen. A lot of Maine's country roads have soft gravel shoulders, so there's not much road for cars and bicycles to share, especially in summer when the traffic gets heavy. That's when bikers should expect to hear a lot of vulgarities directed their way. There was a time when biking was a fairly inexpensive sport, but now with the Day-Glo, skintight suits with padded behinds, fancy bicycle frames, high-tech water bottles, and hospital bills, it's getting costlier by the day.

Camping

Whether you like wilderness camping and cooking over an open fire, or you like 200-channel cable hookups along with

your sewer, water, and electric (just don't confuse them), you'll find both camping styles here in Maine. Camping is a great family activity, especially in Maine where the weather is always warm, it never rains and the bugs are few and far between.

Canoeing

When Europeans first arrived in the New World, they thought the canoe was the cleverest thing they'd ever seen, and after 500 years, canoes are still thought of as a clever way to get around on the water, which, by the way, we have a lot of here in Maine.

From the Saco in the south to the St. John up north, you'll find thousands of places to put in and paddle to your heart's content. Me? I still prefer my boats to have an Evinrude mounted on the stern and a tank of gas on the platform.

Fishing

From freshwater pickerel to saltwater pollock, we've got all kinds of fish. How do you catch one? A local sportsman says: Get your line in the water. Maine has more than 6,000 lakes and ponds and countless miles of rivers, not to mention the Atlantic Ocean. The only thing I don't really get is the whole catch-and-release concept. If I am standing in water all day fighting off bugs or getting seasick in the swells of the ocean, I sure as damn well plan to top that off with a good meal of something I caught.

Hiking

Penny-for-pound it's still the best exercise you can get. Just find a trail somewhere and start walking. Acadia National Park has miles and miles of wonderful trails and Mount Katahdin can be breathtaking. But if you want peace and quiet on the hike, I would head for the North Woods, because Acadia and Baxter State Park can get as crowded as Route 1 on the Fourth of July.

Sea kayaking

If you're thinking of kayaking along Maine's rocky coast, you should keep in mind that lobstermen call kayaks "speed bumps." I don't know what boaters on lakes call them, but it's probably not too nice, either. Kayaking is the water-based equivalent of ultralight flying. To me, you are taking a tiny, semi-stable craft that you have to row and learn to roll with into the Mighty Atlantic, to fend off huge swells, ledges, breakers, boats, and animals. Sign me up!

Skiing

We have to do something in the winter. Cross-country skiing is great if you want to work hard and see some beautiful scenery. Downhill is for people who like to spend gobs of money and have good health insurance.

Whitewater rafting

You're kidding me, right? The only rule in this sport is to try not to drown.

Snowmobiling

Increasingly popular winter activity among natives and NASCAR fans. Maine maintains a complete network of snowmobile trails and businesses that cater to snowmobilers.

Ice fishing

Okay—I think I figured out the basic concept behind ice fishing. Cut a hole in the ice. Place a tent or wooden shake over the hole to keep from freezing to death. Put fishing line through the hole and then get blind-drunk for the weekend. Actually, not a bad concept.

Nightlife

None. (See Las Vegas.)

Shopping

If you're a person who has come to Maine to buy, and we truly hope you are, here's some information to help you decide which of our varied retail offerings is right for you.

Maine Stores

Shopping malls

Like chain motels, the shopping malls in Maine are great if you want to spend money and pretend you don't even know Maine exists. We only have a few of your regular, roofed-over, generic shopping malls in Maine, and it's there you'll find your chain stores, such as those teenage joints that sell, as far as I can tell, only ripped jeans and too-small T-shirts; sporting goods

In our town, the store you gathered in said a lot about your social and economic standing. Certain groups gathered in certain stores; and very few people felt comfortable being "a regular" in more than one of the town's stores. It just wasn't done.

No matter what group in town you belonged to, everyone felt free to go into our local restaurant — The Hungry Boar — but there were rules. You were supposed to sit in the same section and talk to the same people about the same subjects — every friggin' day.

stores that sell dozens of different kinds of what used to be called sneakers; electronic stores with wicked large televisions; and that fancy ladies' underpants place. If you're lucky, the mall will have some big national department stores, too.

Some of my Maine friends swear by the mall, and others just swear at it. I'm not a big mall fan myself, but I think they're good for taking a stroll in during the winter or mud season.

Outlet stores

Maine has some of the best-known outlet shopping areas in the nation: Kittery and Freeport. And if you're the type of person whose heart skips a beat whenever you see a towel or a pair of earrings on sale, or a $250 scarf marked down to $175, you're a prime candidate to visit our "outlet clusters," the most notorious of which are in Kittery (just barely Maine) and Freeport (just barely Freeport).

At outlet stores, *everything* is on sale. No matter that you might be buying factory-second (i.e., chipped or broken) soup bowls, slightly irregular long underwear or, God forbid, last year's jean skirt. The beauty of the outlets is that you won't be paying full price. Or so they say; there are always cynics who say the outlets just print up a jacked-up price label, cross off the price and stick a lower price on.

"Look, Hillary! This designer blouse was $85, but here it's $82.99! Let's each get six!"

Okay, I exaggerate. Sometimes the prices are really good. I once got a pair of deluxe gardening gloves, regularly $10.95, for $2.50. And only one finger was missing.

Maine's outlets are the only reason some people come to Maine. They plan whole vacations going back and forth between Kittery and Freeport and Freeport and Kittery. If this sounds good to you, be our guest.

And Freeport, as most of you undoubtedly know, is home to L.L. Bean, which has a nice store, complete with a trout pond smack dab in the middle. It's not an outlet store, but relax—there is an L.L. Bean outlet in town, too.

Country stores, aka Mom and Pops

Down East and up-country, there are still a few authentic country stores. In the rest of Maine, most of these stores have been bought up by Irving or some other international energy company. But at one time, every Maine town had its version of a country store where half the people in town gather to talk about the other half of the town that isn't there.

While their social function is of the utmost importance, these stores sell a variety of necessary goods like bread, pickled eggs, Slim Jims, bait, milk, Moxie, and pine tree–shaped and –scented air fresheners. The store in my hometown still sells cups of Maxwell House regular. Chain versions of the country store today feature dozens of coffee urns where you can buy a cup of coffee in flavors you wouldn't even put in a bait bag.

In addition to the necessities, these stores are where you'll find some genuine Maine cuisine. Long before McDonalds, these stores were dishing up fast food for harried housewives and single men. Breakfast sandwiches, pizza, spaghetti and meatballs, Italian sandwiches, steamed red hot dogs, whoopie pies, and more are prepared right on the premises. Fresh and good, whatever you get to eat at a Mom and Pop will beat a microwaved burrito from 7-Eleven any day of the week.

There have been some unfortunate developments in the country store world. I was in a small store in Tremont last fall when I saw these two fishermen in line to get coffee. Unfortunately, they were not there just to get regular high-test, but were discussing the merits of Hazelnut versus Chocolate Raspberry and Cinnamon Pumpkin. Sigh; et tu, Wilbur?

Tourist traps

In towns all along the coast there are hundreds of gift shops selling some of the finest and cleverest Maine souvenirs the Chinese have ever made, such as back-scratchers in the shape of lobster claws, pretend moose antlers you can wear on your very own tourist head, and shot glasses imprinted with famous light-houses. These shops are called Tourist Traps—places that draw tourists in and won't release them until they've been tagged and have added a substantial sum to their credit-card debt. You'll know a good tourist trap when you see one—it'll be full of mostly soft-shelled tourists.

Occasionally you'll come upon a store with gifts made here in America. But you'll know it's your lucky day when you come upon a shop that sells gifts that were actually made right here in Maine. They're rare, but like I say, they're out there.

In one coastal town there's a famous gift shop that looks just like a giant lobster trap, the old-fashioned kind with the wooden laths. Come tourist season, wealthy folks—their pockets bulging with ten- and twenty-dollar bills, and of course, credit cards—drive along the lovely coast of Maine, see the giant trap-shaped gift shop and say something like: "Isn't that the most clever thing you ever saw, snookums? We've just got to get a closer look at that place and all the clever items they undoubtedly have inside. Let's park the Volvo and while we're at it, let's plan to spend a pile of these tens and twenties we've been hauling around with us all the way from the city," or words to that effect. You might say they have taken the bait.

Those who aren't familiar with this part of the world may reasonably think that Tourist Traps are a relatively recent development. On the contrary; historians tell us that trapping of one kind or another has been going on around here for some time. Native Americans trapped animals for food and fur. And the first European settlers in this area came just to trap things. Those along our coast trapped haddock and cod; those inland, along our rivers and in our vast forests, trapped things like beaver.

So, for us twenty-first-century folks here in Maine, it's not all that difficult to make the leap from trapping fish and beaver to trapping our summer visitors with deftly designed gift shops.

Of course, tourist traps are a lot more pleasant than animal traps. And the bait in a tourist trap has a more pleasant odor to it—usually something like vanilla from the $15.95 hand-dipped scented candles or balsam from those little $6.50 sachet pillows.

Flea markets

Flea markets were eBay before there was an eBay. And despite the threat of technology, flea markets are still going strong. There are lots of goods moved out of state through flea markets. Of course, there is also a self-perpetuation about flea markets as well, meaning that people basically buy goods at a flea market or yard sale and then just end up reselling the same item at another flea market or yard sale.

But also hanging over every flea market is a dream—a dream of finding a priceless antique amongst the broken mirrors, stained clothes and salvaged tool sets. Indeed, flea markets have something to do with the crazy idea that of all the thousands of people out there wandering around, pawing through tons of worthless junk, you're the only one who's going to find the one-of-a-kind priceless object that when sold will allow you to retire. Too many people watching *Antiques Roadshow*, I guess. Your odds are better with Megabucks—a lot better.

Yard sales

Anthropologists say soon after humans discovered caves, they created yards, or in Maine, dooryards. Soon after that, they devised the first primitive yard sales. You can witness how this primitive activity has survived—yet strangely has not substantially evolved—over the eons if you drive on any road in the entire state from Mud Season through Leaf Season. Yard sales are a good chance to pick up must-have items such as Veg-o-matics, half-sprouted Chia pets, and Ginsu knives that you've seen on TV and always wanted. This is because Mainers spend a lot of time watching TV in the winter months and out of sheer boredom order up everything they see in the infomercials or on

QVC. Consider us to be your personal shoppers: We buy the stuff you really want. And what's more, we sell it to you at a fraction of the price we bought it for, which, of course, was already a fraction of the regular retail price—or at least they said so on TV.

Yard sales offer a lot of other stuff, too. Kids' toys, old sporting goods, exercise bikes, knickknacks, kitchenware, empty Avon bottles. Sometimes there's even furniture to be had. One fella from back home, who lost everything he had, including his trailer, in his fourth and I hope final acrimonious divorce, actually furnished a new apartment from top to bottom from yard sales. Place didn't look all that bad, neither.

There's also a kind of subspecies of yard sales, and that occurs when someone, like a potter or a painter or some other fast-food worker, puts his or her wares out in the yard for sale. This is not a yard sale, per se, you understand, but a sale in the yard. You'll find lots of these along Route 1.

Maine legends: Reny's and Marden's

Many of your larger local stores have gone out of business, but Maine still has some well-known, legendary stores that are based right here in Maine: Reny's and Marden's.

If you like good deals, these are the places for you. If you hate neatly arranged, carefully cleaned aisles, these are the places for you. If you like to be surprised because you never know what they might or might not have in stock—again, these are the places for you.

Both stores are genuine Maine institutions. Reny's has been around since 1949. It's a discount store, and it sells lots of stuff, from brand-name clothing to cans of corn with brands you never heard of. Marden's has been in business for thirty-five years or so, give or take. It's a surplus and salvage store, meaning its buyers swoop down on bankruptcy courts, natural disaster sites and overstocked warehouses and the like, and bring it back here to Maine to sell. If you pick up a nice hunting jacket for sale at Marden's, you may notice the distinct odor of smoke, or a wall calendar with pictures of puppies may look a bit waterlogged or be dated a few years back. But hey, all of the items are inexpensive, I tell you, and every good Mainer knows to check in each week at their local Marden's to see what's new before heading off to shop elsewhere. In fact, in some houses in parts of Maine, the first lullaby a baby hears is the Marden's theme song: "I should have bought it, when I saw it, at Marden's."

Uncle Henry's

Uncle Henry's is another Maine institution—a weekly magazine (basically page after page of classified advertisements) chock-full of items you desperately need or items that you may never have thought about until you stumbled across them in *Uncle Henry's*. The range of items is stunning. In a recent issue you could have bought, and I quote:

> *1978 Chevy El Camino with 4 mounted snow tires. You tow, runs good for $650.*
>
> *My mother's very expensive Mink coat. 3/4 length, would make beautiful teddy bears. First $50 cash takes it.*
>
> *Composted horse manure and shaving mix. Call for details.*
>
> *Six cans Freon.*
>
> *Richard Simmons, Golden Deal-a-Meal tapes and VCR tapes, asking $50.*
>
> *1985 Oxford 14 x 72 single-wide, 2 bdr, 1 bath, new frig, dishwasher, woodstove, monitor heat, nice cond. You move it. $10,000.*
>
> *15 Adult DVDs 36 hrs long, high-quality, new in package, $100.*
>
> *Huge Elvis bust, excellent cond. The King. $100.*
>
> *Avon Christmas plates, beautiful condition, orig. boxes, 1974 to 2004, asking $500.*

Maine Items

Sometimes it is not the store that you need to know about— it is the item. There are some wonderful categories of items that you should always be on the lookout for when traveling in Maine.

Coffee tables

Mainers have taken coffee tables to a new art form. You can keep your common rectangular wooden coffee tables. Here in Maine you can get a lobster trap that has been turned into a coffee table, a coffee table that doubles as a cribbage board, or a giant spool of wire that has been turned into a coffee table. You name it, we can turn it into a coffee table for you.

Moose poop

Now this is classy. Nothing says I love you like some moose poop jewelry. Some stores sell moose poop candy. Do not be dismayed, they're just joshing you; it's not really excrement at all. The jewelry is though.

Lawn ornaments

Mainers take lawn ornaments to a whole other level. It's an art form, really, one that the rest of the country will catch on to eventually. We've got lawn art to suit any taste, from the bent-over lady with the, ahem, broad south end, to St. Francis bird-baths, to any species of animal made of Styrofoam, to ceramic kitties to wind socks to whirligigs to fake wells to old lobster buoys to rusted washing machines to cars on blocks to pink flamingos to wooden ducks with wings that spin in the wind. You should pick up a few on your travels through the state. They make dandy souvenirs for the lawn ornament-less folks back home, and those recipients will not only be delighted with the gift, they'll be some impressed with your new and cutting-edge taste in art.

Chain saw sculptures

Speaking of cutting-edge, you got nothing, mister man,
until you have decorated your home or yard with an honest-to-
gosh piece of wooden sculpture carved entirely with a chain saw.
Let's see the Chinese knock off cheap imitations of these!
Whether a bear or a moose or a mermaid, the choices are good
and plentiful. Just strap one to the top of your Lexus and haul
it out of here.

Destinations

Spend any time in Maine and you'll eventually hear someone say that everything in Maine is changing fast and
nothing's like it used to be. When I go up the coast to visit the
town I was raised in, the land looks the same but everything
else has changed. If you had visited Maine years ago instead of
now, you would have seen quite a different place.

Like Grover's Corners in Thornton Wilder's *Our Town,* we
had our hometown newspaper. As newspapers go it wasn't
much, and people were always complaining that it didn't carry
much "real" news. But everyone in town read it every week
from cover to cover. Today our town paper is much more
sophisticated and worldly, and reviews things like newly
released DVDs.

Our town always had its town drunk. But because our town
was smaller than most, we couldn't afford a full-time town
drunk. Ours was only part-time. The rest of the time he taught
poetry at the local community college.

Today in our town there are more drunks and more in rehab. There are also more drugs and the social problems they foster.

While writing this book I've spent more time than usual thinking about my hometown and how it's changed over the years—and how *all* Maine towns have changed. I've also been wondering what kind of a play Thornton Wilder would have written if his play was set in a New England town of the twenty-first century.

 If you are pressed for time, try to adhere to the MLL rule— Moose, Lobster, and Lighthouse. According to the MLL rule, all visitors to Maine should plan to see a moose, eat a lobster, and be photographed next to a lighthouse. Some eccentric tourists will sometimes mix things up by eating a moose, being photographed with a lobster, and just seeing a lighthouse. Any combination of nouns and verbs is acceptable as long as no local decency statutes are violated and you manage—in some way—to include a moose, a lobster, and a lighthouse in your visit.

I can imagine it now. In the part of the play where the town is described, a Stage Manager might say something like this:

"There's our elementary school over there. You might be interested in knowing it's now a Drug-Free Zone. We're very proud of those new signs out front. And so far this year, we haven't had but two or three weapons found on kids as they went through the metal detector there in the school.

'Course, the year isn't quite over yet.

"Ever since the Wal-Mart opened just outside of town on the old Indian burial ground, there are fewer businesses here on Main Street, but over there at the end of that row of empty stores is our fancy new, talking and bilingual ATM installed by some giant Boston bank. First mugging's gonna take place there in about five months.

"Further along Main Street is our all-night Gas-n-Go convenience store. You wouldn't believe the seedy characters and career reprobates that gather there to eat microwave burritos and hoot 'n' holler all hours of the day and night. Police tend to like it, though. They say a place like that helps by keeping all the town's usual suspects in one place.

"We have a tanning salon in our town. Why anyone would want to destroy the natural pasty-white winter complexion most Mainers have and pay good money to replace it with a strange-looking, shoe-polish-brown complexion is beyond me. But some people seem to like it.

"Our reproductive health clinic is over there next to the adult video store. And our methadone clinic is just across the street."

Yes, things have changed here in Maine.

Acadia National Park

Highest elevation: Cadillac Mountain, 1,530 feet.

There are beautiful state parks throughout Maine where a lot of nice walking is done, and then there's our only national park—Acadia—where you can hike to your heart's content through some of the most spectacular scenery on the planet.

Acadia was one of the first national parks in the nation and came about, among many other reasons, because of what is called enlightened self-interest. Around the turn of the twentieth century, all the zillionaires who summered on Mount Desert Island became alarmed when too many (to their mind, anyway) middle-class types and general riffraff also began building houses or summer homes on their special island. The zillionaires wanted to put a quick end to such foolishness, while teaching the riffraff a little about knowing their place. Their place, the zillionaires were quick to agree, was definitely *not* anywhere near them on Mount Desert.

So, before the middle class could establish a stronger foothold, the enlightened wealthy people moved quickly to buy up tens of thousands of acres of prime real estate, including miles of oceanfront, and turned all that real estate over to the federal government with strict instructions to turn the whole plot into the national park we all enjoy today. Yes, riffraff can visit it, too, but to the zillionaire's mind, at least they're not moving in next door.

The Allagash

Ask someone about the Allagash, and they'll most likely say, "Huh?" The Allagash is the name of both a town (pop. 277) and a wilderness waterway in Aroostook County. The Allagash waterway is known as one of the wildest places in Maine, second only to the Old Port in Portland.

The Allagash is so wild and so remote, not many people have been there. The people who've been there would probably be hard-pressed to find it again.

It's worth looking for, though. Maybe you should leave some bread crumbs behind you, though, just in case.

Aroostook County

Aroostook, Maine's largest and quirkiest county, was incorporated in 1839, and some say it's been all downhill ever since. Around here Aroostook is known simply as The County, in the same way that New York is The City and certain summer visitors are The Problem.

Even though The County is made up of over 6,672 square miles, it can barely claim 74,000 residents, according to the latest census. And the way people are packing up and leaving, that may well be down below 70,000 by the time this book is out.

The County has just under 6 percent of the state's population and there are 11.1 persons per square mile. They say .1 because every square mile or so you'll find someone who isn't all there.

With all that land it only has 2 cities, 54 towns, 11 plantations, and 108 unorganized townships. Mostly, The County is famous for its potatoes, but other major crops include broccoli, buckwheat, hay, and small grain rotation crops. Aroostook is very proud of its snowmobile season. It should be. It lasts from September to June, sometimes longer.

 An Aroostook potato farmer walked into the unemployment office in Presque Isle one summer morning and told the person at the desk that he needed fifty experienced ho-ahs.

A little confused, the clerk asked the farmer to repeat his request.

"I need fifty ho-ahs," the farmer said, a little annoyed. "I was told I could find all the ho-ahs I needed here at your office."

"Ho-ahs," the clerk asked. "Do you mean prostitutes?"

"I don't care nothing about what religion they are, so long as they can hoe potatoes," the farmer said.

Augusta (state capital)
Pop.: 18,631

Our state capital straddles the mighty Kennebec River, which incidentally, flows out of Moosehead Lake (see Greenville). Much of Augusta has all the charm of a strip mall, but there are wonderful spots. Two of the best reasons to visit Augusta are the Maine State Museum and Old Fort Western.

Bangor
Pop.: 31,473

Bangor, sometimes know as Lewiston without the frills, is the unofficial capital of Eastern Maine. People come from all over the Greater Bangor Metropolitan Area to shop, eat at fancy restaurants like McDonalds and Wendy's, attend events and look at vacant buildings. Historically, Bangor was once the largest lumber port in the world due in part to its position at the headwaters of the Penobscot River. Most of the lumber that came out of the North Woods flowed down the Penobscot and was shipped from Bangor ports. At the time, Bangor was also known for its bars and brothels. In tribute to its lumbering legacy, Bangor is also the proud home of one of the world's largest Paul Bunyan statues, a 31-foot-tall, 1.5-ton sculpture that ranks right up there with Michelangelo's David and the lesser-known Cherryfield's Vernon. The statue stands on Main Street next to the Bangor Auditorium, which was originally built to provide shelter to the folks attending public executions in winter.

In a related gory subject, Bangor is probably best known these days for being the hometown of best-selling horror writer Stephen King. But if I were you, I wouldn't hang around outside his home waiting to catch a glimpse of this famous guy. The last tourist known to have done so—well, let's just say that truth is sometimes stranger than fiction.

Bar Harbor
Pop.: 2,680

Often confused with Acadia National Park. Much of old—
i.e., *rich*—Bar Harbor burned in the Great Fire of 1947. Since
that time it has alternately been recast as a T-shirt and junk
store center, a mecca of New Age stores, an "art" center and,
most recently, it has been taken over by hotels. Bar Harbor is
undeniably beautiful, though.

Warning: If you are traveling on a budget, avoid Bar
Harbor at all costs in the summer.

Bath
Pop.: 9,394

Since the first ship built in the New World, the *Virginia*,
was built right near Bath at Popham Beach in 1607, the folks
on the Kennebec will celebrate 400 years of shipbuilding in
2007. Most of that shipbuilding went on in and around the city
of Bath, home of Bath Iron Works and the Maine Maritime
Museum.

Bath is also the home of Ed's Barber Shop located on fashionable Front Street. Ed can tell you more about Bath than I
can, so stop by for a haircut and a story.

Baxter State Park

The 205,000 acres—give or take a square foot or two—that
make up Baxter State Park were a gift to the people of Maine
from one of our more enlightened politicians, Governor Percival
P. Baxter. This extraordinary man felt that Mount Katahdin and
its surroundings should belong to the people of Maine for all gen-
erations. Having spent years in Maine politics, Baxter knew right
off that his colleagues in Augusta wouldn't Git-R-Done—as they

say—so in 1931 he began doing it himself. He bought the land with his own money and then set up trust funds to support its management. Once all the heavy lifting and tedious paperwork was finished, the Legislature accepted as state property the land commonly known as Mount Katahdin and the South Basin.

Dante said: "Midway through life's journey, I went astray from the true road and found myself alone in a dark wood." People round here think he was talking about the North Woods.

Again, not trusting our Legislature to care for his gift and manage his trust funds, Governor Baxter created the Baxter State Park Authority, which was given the task of managing his exquisite park and keeping it out of politicians' hands.

Trust funds and user fees support the park, which—to this day—does not draw a single penny from the state's general fund. As Governor Baxter said, "There is no room for politics within the management of this park."

To find out more about this special place, go to: www.baxterstateparkauthority.com, or just head for the park office on Balsam Drive in Millinocket. The folks there can tell you all about it, and they'll even give you brochures and maps if you ask them nicely.

Beaches

"Does Maine even have beaches?" many of you will ask, often sarcastically.

Until summer visitors started poking around asking such snide questions, most Maine people didn't give much thought to it. Beaches? I guess we have beaches. You just may have trouble seeing them because they're covered with rocks, not your typical, run-of-the-mill sand.

Thousand of years ago when that mile-high glacier started sliding over Maine at about a foot a year (which is just a tad slower than summer traffic moves through Wiscasset today), it was very generous, liberally scattering rocks of every shape, size, and type. The more massive of these rocks eventually became what we now call the rocky coast of Maine.

The one thing the glacier neglected to leave us in any great quantity was beach sand. Oh, sure, there's Popham Beach, Pine Point Beach, Old Orchard Beach, Wells Beach, and a few others that are sandy, but they're the exceptions that prove the rule.

Maine has three thousand miles of tidal oceanfront, and our beaches take up only a few of those miles. Yeah, we know all about the miles and miles of white sandy beaches our southern neighbors have. We've all heard of—and believe it or not some

Ten Actual Maine Place Names

Pronounce them at your peril.
1. Chemquasabamticook Lake (Piscataquis County)
2. Eskutassis Pond (Penobscot County)
3. Lazygut Island (Hancock County)
4. Mattamiscontis Township (Penobscot County)
5. Mooselookmeguntic Lake (Oxford County)
6. Passagassawakeag River (forms part of Belfast Harbor)
7. Pennamaquam Lake (Washington County)
8. Sysladobsis Lake (Penobscot County)
9. Yankeetuladi Pond (Aroostook County)
10. Mosquito Island (Knox County)

of us have even visited—the beaches of Cape Cod, and even tiny Rhode Island.

A lot of Mainers handle the lack of sand beaches by making a personal decision early in life never to go swimming. In fact, most lobstermen who spend their lives on the water have never gone in the water and do everything they can to avoid that.

My friend Earl Pease once said, "If I fall in that forty-degree water dressed in my gear, a wool shirt, lined jeans, boots, and cap, I'd be froze to death and headed for the bottom before I had time to take two strokes, even if I knew how to make two strokes. So why bother?"

Back home our family had two places to swim—one for high tide and one for low. At high tide we'd swim right off the rocks near the house. At low water you had to slip over barnacles and seaweed to get to the water, so we'd drive to a beach about five miles away. Eventually we got a wharf and a float in front of our place and could swim there no matter what the tide.

But some of my fondest childhood memories involve long summer days at the low tide beach when we would bring hot dogs and hamburgers to cook. Being a good Maine beach, there were lots of trees to sit under and lots of crevasses in nearby rocks for building fires.

Such beach events had to be planned well in advance so you'd have time to arrive and set up on the outgoing tide and then have several hours to cook and eat and swim before the tide returned and took the whole beach back.

Special Note: Old Orchard Beach is the closest thing our state has to a traditional seaside resort, and it has the industrial-strength fried dough, tacky trinkets, vulgar T-shirt shops, gaudy amusement park, tattoo parlors, and bars, bars, and more bars to prove it. Some of you may like that. But be advised: Old

Orchard is way down south in York County, which, as we've said, may as well be New Hampshire or Massachusetts.

Belfast
Pop.: 6,381

Once known for its poultry industry, Belfast was largely invaded by financial giant MBNA during the 1980s and '90s. Also known as the place where you make a left turn from Route 3 onto Route 1 when you are heading for Bar Harbor.

Bethel
Pop.: 2,536

Right here in 1999, residents built Angus, the World's Tallest Snowman. You can look it up.

Boothbay Harbor
Pop.: 1,237

Never been there. Heard it's nice.

Brunswick
Pop.: 14,816

Home to Bowdoin College and all those spoiled rich kids, Brunswick also boasts of having the former home of Civil War hero General Joshua Lawrence Chamberlain, perhaps Maine's greatest hero of all time. Even better, you can also eat at the aptly named drive-in restaurant, Fat Boys, which still features carhops.

Bucksport
Pop.: 2,970

One of my favorite Maine ghost stories comes from the Hancock County town of Bucksport. You've got to like the story, or more honestly, stories, they tell about how the black shape of a foot and part of a shapely leg ended up on the otherwise unblemished granite gravestone of Colonel Jonathan Buck—the Revolutionary War hero and founder of the town. The mark is there and it's distinctive. I've seen it. And I've heard they've tried to wash the darned thing off a number of times. It always returns.

Anyway, most agree the foot-and-leg marking is a curse of some kind—but who cast it, and why?

Some say it was a leg and foot left by a high-stepping chorus girl whom the colonel once dated. But historians dismiss such an explanation, reminding us that although ol' Buck did have an eye for the ladies and would undoubtedly have dated a shapely-gammed chorus girl if given the chance, there were, unfortunately for the colonel, no chorus girls—shapely-gammed or otherwise—living in Bucksport at the time.

Another story says it was the result of a curse put on Buck by a woman he sentenced to death for practicing witchcraft. In one version, while she's burning to death in a fire ordered set by Buck, her son yanks off her leg and hits Buck with it. Ouch! For both of them!

Folks in Bucksport will be glad to tell you any number of stories behind the mysterious gravestone foot. Who knows which one is nearest the truth, or even if any of them are? The only known truth is that the ghostly foot exists.

Calais
Pop.: 3,447

I believe this town is now part of Canada, but I'll check.

Camden/Rockland
Pop.: 3,934 / 7,666

The ditty goes:
Camden by the sea,
Rockland by the smell,
Thomaston's a good old town
And Warren's gone to hell.

A bootlegged version goes:
Camden by the sea,
Rockland by the smell
But if you want to get to Hell fast
Go to Belfast.

It's unknown who wrote the verse, but I'm thinking it probably wasn't Camden native and noted poet Edna St. Vincent Millay. And I doubt it was the local organizer of the BELFAST IS FOR LOVERS publicity campaign.

Anyway, Camden and Rockland are linked like twins, at least in name. Camden (setting for the infamous Peyton Place), with its hills, has always been the ritzier of the four towns. Rockland used to be noted for the distinct odors coming from its various fishing operations. Now, even Rockland has been yuppified, if that's still a word, and chichi coffee shops and upscale clothing stores abound right there along the water. And, of course, it's the site of the Maine Lobster Festival, PETA's favorite annual event.

As for the other two towns in the verse, well, there's not much to mention. Thomaston was once home to the Maine State Prison, and Warren wasn't known for much except Warren Days. Oh, and the home of Crowe Rope.

Caribou
Pop.: 8,312

Caribou was settled by soldiers who went to fight in the Aroostook War of 1838–39 and then apparently got lost and couldn't find their way home. Now it's a business center of Aroostook County.

Castine
Pop.: 1,143

Wabanaki for "Place that is down a long peninsula and very hard to get to and not much there anyway." Home of Maine Maritime Academy.

Cherryfield
Pop.: 1,157

My hometown is known to one and all as "The Jewel of the Narraguagus." What Bangor once was to the pine board, the small town of Cherryfield still is to the blueberry. And please don't ask why the world's Blueberry Capital has "cherry" in its name. For one thing, it's not that great of a story, and for another, you don't really need to know things like that.

Eastport
Pop.: 1,640

Located on Moose Island in Passamaquoddy Bay. Hey, that's kinda cool, no?

Ellsworth
Pop.: 6,456

Privately owned rest area for people heading to Acadia National Park.

Farmington
Pop.: 4,098

Shiretown of Franklin County and hometown of Chester Greenwood (1858–1937), the man who invented earmuffs. Greenwood invented the first pair of ear protectors when he was just fifteen. The town now celebrates Chester Greenwood Day in his honor on the first day of winter. Seriously.

Fort Kent
Pop.: 1,978

Located roughly a twenty-day drive from Portland, it's just about as far north as you can go in Maine. Fort Kent is separated from Canada by the St. John River and helps protect the United States from hostile invasion by crazy hockey players.

Freeport
Pop.: 1,813

In the process of being renamed L.L. Beanville.

And, for some reason, Freeport is home to an honest-to-goodness desert.

Fryeburg
Pop.: 3,292

One of the nicest towns in western Maine, Fryeburg comes to life every fall to host one of our oldest and largest fairs—The Fryeburg Fair, a production of the West Oxford Agricultural

Society. And, you can be sure the Fryeburg Fair is teeming with fried dough; hence, the town's name.

Greenville/Moosehead Lake
Pop.: 1,319

I was going to say Greenville sits at the bottom of Moosehead Lake, but that might give you the wrong idea. It's actually at the southern tip of Maine's largest lake (32 miles long and 5 miles wide at its widest point), and it's the closest thing to a bustling town you'll come to in that area. But, then, they say people go up to Moosehead to get away from all the hustle and bustle, so there you go—or you should.

From summer to fall, hunting to snowmobiling, Greenville is just a beehive of activity. Things slow down a bit during Mud Season, but that's about the only rest it gets.

Jackman
Pop.: 718

If Maine has a back door, it's hanging on its hinges in Jackman where many people who don't like front doors cross over into Canada. Where's Maine's front door? Good question. Kittery, I guess.

Kennebunkport
Pop.: 4,804

Believe it or not, some tourists opt to bypass Sanford and head right for historic Kennebunkport, which may be the most expensive town in Maine, in order to get in a line of traffic and drive by the summer home of the first President George Bush on Walker's Point. Then they stop in Dock Square to purchase some of the most overpriced merchandise on the planet.

Dock Square is also the site of the infamous shopkeeper riots and tourist protests of 2002–03. Yes, I said riots, and it all started when town officials began getting complaints from wealthy, well-connected residents annoyed by all the large exhaust-spewing motor coaches that came to town and parked with their engines running as their passengers, i.e., you tourists, walked around and shopped for an hour or two.

In other words, these Kennebunkport residents objected to red-blooded Americans engaging in commerce, the purest and most patriotic of all American activities.

In response to the complaints, the town council initiated a fee for coaches wanting to park in town. The fee angered the coach owners who said they'd boycott the town rather than pay it. Taking an idea from another turbulent time in American history, some bus drivers wanted to dump their buses in Kennebunkport Harbor in protest, but that idea didn't get far.

Anyway, when coach owners said they'd no longer stop, coach passengers were angered, realizing that they would be denied the opportunity to shop for overpriced Chinese-made Maine souvenirs in Kennebunkport's expensive shoppes.

When the coaches stopped coming, the shopkeepers were up in arms at the loss of tourist business.

Things got ugly for a while. Angry mobs of tourists were gathering in Dock Square and pouring out their $6 skinny-mocha lattes in protest. Coach drivers equipped their coaches with mag wheels and began drag racing up and down Main Street to show their displeasure with the fee.

Eventually, the merchants prevailed, the fee was dropped, the coaches returned, filled with tourists, and a type of peace settled over Kennebunkport—for the time being.

Kittery

Pop.: 5,884

This historic town was originally settled in 1623, but in the 1980s was officially converted into a shopping center.

Lewiston/Auburn

Pop.: 35,690
Pop.: 23,203

It is against the law in Maine to mention these two towns separately. Once the center of mill industry, the towns fell on hard times and are now bouncing back. We love the promotional campaign that pegs Lewiston and Auburn as the "LA" area. Add some sun, some jobs, and some movie stars and you would swear you were in Southern California. Honest.

Lisbon Falls

Pop.: 4,420

Home of Moxie.

Lubec

Pop.: 1,610

Once a thriving center for packing sardines. The late home of the state's Vacant Building Festival. We now believe this town has been abandoned entirely.

Madawaska

Pop.: 3,326

Has a mill.

Mexico
Pop.: 2,969

Mexico is one of the bigger cities in the middle of nowhere, also known as Western Maine. It has nothing in common with its more southern namesake, except maybe for its water.

Ogunquit
Pop.: 1,281

Another town at the pointy end of the state, Ogunquit is noted for its arts colony, which dates back to the 1890s and produced some of America's most famous artists. I can't recall which ones at the moment, but I'm sure someone down there can tell you. It's also known for its summer theater and for Perkins Cove, which, with its high-priced shoppes, is a lot like Dock Square (see Kennebunkport), only harder to get in and out of.

Old Orchard Beach
Pop.: 8,856

Maine's token honky-tonk region. Lots of bars, beaches, and the highest per capita amount of tacky clothing and gift items in the state.

Portland
Pop.: 64,249

Maine's most self-important city. With 60,000 residents, give or take—and most of them take—Portland is by far Maine's largest city. It's really a lot bigger than that, when you count all the unfortunate folks who live in what is called the Greater Portland Metropolitan Area.

Most Mainers dislike Portland because there's lots to dislike about it. It's got lots of lawyers working there, for one thing.

The waterfront really reeks when the fleets dock. You have to pay to park on the streets, for Pete's sake. And, lately, the city's been on this kick about developing its "Arts District." By this it appears they mean recruiting lots of young folks with pink and green hair and pierced body parts to hang out on upper Congress Street. Who knows?

But still, there's always something going on in this big city, so you won't be bored if you have to visit it. The theater, the symphony, museums, art galleries—all those stuffy things are there to be had.

Presque Isle
Pop.: 9,511

A place in Aroostook County that is home to the only open-all-night tourist center in Northern Maine. Now, that's progress.

Rangeley
Pop.: 1,113

This must be one racy little town because it is home to the Wilhelm Reich Museum. Reich was a psychiatrist, psychoanalyst and scientist who had some complicated theories that even I don't understand, about energy forces and so on. Now don't tell anyone I told you, but energy of a sexual nature had a lot to do with those theories. (One day I'm going to go check out that museum when my wife's not around.) I think Reich was eventually thrown in jail, but you can find out all about that and his greater pile of work at his museum.

Other than that, Rangeley is a very pretty little place on a lake with mountains.

Sebago Lake

Jet ski racetrack.

Skowhegan
Pop.: 6,696

Birthplace of Margaret Chase Smith.

Wiscasset
Pop.: 1,203

Wiscasset has been voted the Prettiest Village in Maine by someone. It's on the sign. But Wiscasset is perhaps best known for what no longer is there to be seen. Several years ago, two old ships were unceremoniously removed from the waterfront after it was determined that they were public safety hazards to those on land who liked to climb on them, and that they were a navigational hazard to vessels on the water that had to navigate around them.

The two old, 200-foot, four-masted schooners were the *Luther Little* and the *Hesper*, abandoned on the banks of the Sheepscot (Maine's prettiest riverbank) in 1932 because—according to their owners—the ships had nothing to haul, it being the Great Depression and all.

Now that the quaint ships are gone, Wiscasset boasts of being the home of Red's Eats (Maine's prettiest take-out stand) and the Old Lincoln County Jail (Maine's first and still prettiest pokey.)

What few people these days know about Wiscasset is that it was once Maine's chief port, until Congress passed the Embargo Act of 1807 and managed to cripple trade in the seaport.

Wiscasset was also the homeport of the colorful Captain Clough who—they say—once brought back to Wiscasset from one of his trips to the Orient the ancestor of the "coon cat" (Maine's prettiest cat).

York
Pop.: 13,538

Former Maine town invaded and repossessed by Massachusetts. Today it is part of the Greater Boston Metropolitan statistical area.

Goodbye: Come Again!

If you find that your motel room isn't what you expected or the cabin on the lake doesn't look exactly like the brochure or the online photo, please don't complain. No one likes a whiner.

In the mid-1940s, my parents bought a camp on four wooded acres right on the water. All through my childhood we spent summers there. Out-of-staters would call it a summer cottage, but we called it our camp. The family would head to camp soon after school closed in June and wouldn't return to our winter house until the day after Labor Day.

Some of my fondest childhood memories involve the summer days we spent at camp. And then there were "laundry days."

But before we get to that grim topic, let me tell you a little more about the place. Conditions at camp during the early years were a bit primitive, but things did manage to get better each year.

In the beginning there was a hand pump at the kitchen sink and a pipe that ran from the pump straight down to the cool, clear spring in the cellar. To get something as simple as a glass of water you'd stand there at the sink and pump it right out of the spring. All cooking was done on the Home Clarion wood-stove in the kitchen. We also had a Franklin stove to heat the sitting room, or den. There were six rooms and all were furnished in what you might call Down East rustic. Since the prevailing winds were out of the southwest, our outhouse sat in a grove of trees about 50 feet from the northeast corner of the camp.

Eventually, Bangor Hydro Electric got around to running wires up to the area around our camp, and things changed pretty radically.

My father had a well drilled beside the house, and before long we had hot and cold running water for the first time. The hand pump was then replaced by a shiny new kitchen sink with dazzling chrome spigots. The old black Home Clarion was retired and a sparkling white General Electric took its place.

It was decided that the Franklin would remain on duty in the den.

I don't know how our laundry was handled in the days before electricity, but after the wires went in my folks got one of the strangest-looking washing machines I ever saw, before or since. It looked and acted like something Jules Verne might have designed while on some strong hallucinogenic substance.

I was about five or six at the time, and to the best of my recollection this strange device consisted of a huge copper tank on wheels which would have come up to about my chin if I had dared get close enough to it to measure. On laundry day my mother would wheel the contentious-looking device out of its dark corner, fill it with water from the sink and then put in the clothes and the laundry soap.

Agitation for the wash cycle was provided by four metal suction cups that would go up and down and swing alternately and violently from left to right. As foreboding as this rig looked while it was at rest, it became downright menacing when my mother plugged it in and switched the monster on. The floor of our camp would begin shaking as this frothing monster came alive and the suction cups began thrashing about in the soapy, turbulent water.

I don't know how long we had this strange clothes washer. It may not have been an entire season. But memories of it have remained with me now for over half a century.

Since this was America where progress, they say, is our most important product, things had to change. Eventually a modern new laundry opened in a town 10 miles from our camp. It was a tiny place in a narrow storefront filled with automatic washers. The idea was to drop off your bags of dirty clothes in the morning and when you returned in the afternoon, everything would be washed, fluff-dried and folded.

Each week we'd load the bags of laundry into the back of the station wagon and drive to town.

I remember the woman who ran this hectic operation always had wet, stringy curls drooping down over her chubby face. She stood in the middle of her domain surrounded by mountains of dirty laundry brought in by half the people in the county, but she always seemed so jolly. Even as a kid I wondered how she kept each order separate. Apparently she didn't. Each week a few of our items didn't return with our load but strange items of clothing did.

We didn't complain. Considering the alternative, we probably would have carried those laundry bags to town on our backs.

If you had talked to us back then of today's digital, programmable "home laundry systems," we would have assumed you were drunk.

You are now leaving our fair state. Thanks for coming.

But, Seriously Folks

Seriously, though, folks, Maine is a unique and fantastic place to visit (why else would we have named it Vacationland), and I encourage you to take in as much of the state as possible from Fort Kent to Calais to Kittery. Every town and every region has something special to offer—much of it you will not find anywhere else in America.

Please check out the sources below for some information that will actually be helpful. Heck, you can even drop me an e-mail if you want, and I may be able to recommend a great place to eat or visit. Just send a note to mainestoryteller@yahoo.com.

Maine Office of Tourism	www.visitmaine.com
State of Maine	www.maine.gov
Maine Tourism Association	www.mainetourism.com
Acadia National Park	www.nps.gov/acad
Maine Department of Transportation	www.exploremaine.org
Maine Innkeepers Association	www.maineinns.com
Maine Campground Owners Association	www.campinmaine.com

John McDonald

Above all else, John McDonald loves to tell stories (some might say he just loves to talk, but we digress!) about the people and places of Maine, from Eastport to Kittery and from Fort Kent to Frenchboro.

John performs at events throughout Maine and New England and has done so for decades, constantly perfecting his unique brand of Maine storytelling and humor in front of audiences large and small.

His previous book, *A Moose and a Lobster Walk Into a Bar*, was a smash hit, topping best-seller lists at bookstores throughout Maine and introducing him to people across the nation.

John also writes a weekly humor column and hosts a weekend radio show on WGAN AM-560.

Previously, he worked as a reporter at newspapers in Rhode Island and Maine and is a graduate of Providence College. He lives in Portland.

To inquire about hiring John for a storytelling or book event, please call 207-688-6290, e-mail info@islandportpress.com or visit www.islandportpress.com.